TWICE SAVED: A QUIET MIRACLE

God's Incredible Healing and His Amazing Plan for an Ordinary Man

By: Rich Hall

DISCLAIMER

Opinions expressed in this book are those of the author and do not necessarily represent the opinions of the California Department of Corrections and Rehabilitation, Federal Bureau of Prisons, or Department of Justice.

To all those struggling to overcome drug addiction, self-destructive behavior, debilitating shame, or life-limiting doubt; may you find the hope you need to move forward toward the meaningful existence God has planned for you.

To all the program participants who permitted me into their lives and trusted enough to allow God's healing to reach them as He worked in our groups.

AUTHOR'S NOTE

Everything presented in this story is based on my best recollection of the events described. Every attempt was made to avoid embellishment or dramatization. What is written here is, to the best of my ability, an accurate record of what really happened.

To protect the privacy of individuals I have worked with, any mention of a particular drug treatment participant or description of a specific incident involving a program participant may be a compilation of several similar participants or events encountered over the years. Descriptions of coworkers include altered personal characteristics, including but not limited to position of employment.

CONTENTS

INTRODUCTION

"If God has done something wonderful in your life, share it with others."

These simple words included in a daily devotional inspired me to write this book. For several years I considered writing an account of the events that shaped my life, but it wasn't until I read this phrase that I felt spiritually called to share this story with others.

So what is it I have to share? This is a story about addiction and recovery, about human failure and Divine redemption. It is an account of a broken man being lifted up, falling back down, only to be lifted up again. And it is a narrative about faith and perseverance in following God's will even when unsure where it is leading. Mostly though, it is a story about a miracle; a quiet miracle involving a twice-lost man and how God has used him to help a small group of neglected, frequently abused, and mostly forgotten people.

This story focuses specifically on Jesus Christ working in, and through, the life of an ordinary person. It contains no mention of a lavish lifestyle gone wrong, provides no juicy tidbits about celebrity or fame, and does not involve a famous athlete, entertainer, or politician. It is my hope that the absence of such distracting matters enhances the story, making it more personal and authentic. For the true value of this story--my story--is that it could easily be yours, or your mom or dad's, your aunt's, your little sister's, or even your child's. Nothing included here is unique to my life. Everything I experienced, both the suffering due to my own failures and the miracle of God's intervention, could happen to anyone.

This book is not intended to be a detailed account of my life. I've included only experiences that add to the purpose of this writing, because really, this book is not about me. It is about the awesome healing power and love of Jesus Christ and the plans He has for each of us. I simply serve as a witness to the way God uses common people--even hurting and broken people--to bring about His will. I wrote this book to share with others this truth about Him.

I hope this writing provides encouragement to people who worry that past or present sin renders them unworthy of God's love and forgiveness. I also hope it encourages those who doubt He has a plan for them and inspires others who believe there is no place in their simple lives for God to do good works.

God is awesome. He does miraculous--if not always spectacular--things in our lives every day. Ideally, I would be able to sit down with you and personally share how he has done so in my life, but until such an opportunity presents itself this book will have to suffice. In the following pages I will share the wonderful things He has done in, and through, my life.

PART 1
Saved From the Depths

CHAPTER 1

A Steady Descent

For a kid living in southern California during the 1970s, drinking beer or smoking marijuana was about as common as carrying a cell phone is for young people today. At least that was the case with the kids I knew where I grew up. So when I began getting high (smoking pot and drinking beer) at age 12 it just seemed like the thing to do. The common refrain uttered by adolescents for decades, "Everyone I know is doing it", was mostly true for me.

I took an immediate and powerful liking to smoking pot and I found I had a high tolerance for alcohol and loved the way both substances made me feel. Almost from the start I became a daily user. I quickly learned that getting high could help me get through uncomfortable situations in my life. When I was bored it gave me something to do. When I was anxious it helped me calm down. And when I was scared or unsure of myself, it gave me confidence.

One of the more significant benefits I discovered about getting high was how drinking impacted me socially. Though I had friends and didn't noticeably stand out as being awkward, inwardly I always felt uncomfortable in social situations. But when I started smoking pot and drinking with other kids, for the first time I felt like I belonged. Additionally, there were some issues at home that weren't much fun to deal with and I soon found that getting high before going home made things there a little more tolerable.

Though getting high proved to be quite useful, the benefits didn't come without a cost. Of course I didn't see it at the time, but years later, while in treatment and then later still while studying addiction in college, I learned that by relying on a mood-altering substance to cope I was failing to develop the life skills which most kids learn, however awkwardly, during their teen years.

I was never given a substance abuse assessment back then, but if I had been given one which focused on issues of control, tolerance, and withdrawal (as many do) I would have almost certainly been diagnosed with a substance abuse disorder by the age of 14 and maybe even earlier. Despite this, I finished junior high seeing myself as not all that different from the kids I ran around with. This would change during high school as I began to recognize that I was partying more than most of the other kids.

Going into high school I was a pretty good athlete. As a kid I was a good basketball player, but quit playing in junior high because practice got in the way of partying with my friends. Once in high school I decided to play football and wrestle during my freshmen year. I enjoyed both, but by 10th grade my interest in getting high completely overwhelmed any interest I had in either of these two sports. Despite my growing interest with partying, I did continue to play baseball, something I had done well since age seven or eight. I played all four years of high school and was the Captain of the team during my senior season.

During this time I thought of myself first and foremost as a baseball player. I even had aspirations of someday being a pro ballplayer. The problem was I often partied before games and though back then I would have insisted that it in no way hindered my ability to play, I'm now confident that being frequently buzzed negatively impacted my level of play on the field.

Outside of baseball all I did in high school was party. My grades were unremarkable and, actually, quite forgettable. In fact I don't remember any, good or bad. All I know is that I graduated on time with my class. What I do remember is in the last couple of years, particularly after my dad died on the last day of tenth grade, I drank pretty much every day, including before school and as soon as I got out at lunch time.

My dad's passing was tough and I don't doubt it hit me harder than I recognized at the time (I never really grieved, I just kind of went on with life), but I have never considered it a major factor in my drinking. The truth is by the time he died my course had been charted; I was addicted long before his death.

During high school I had plenty of friends and a steady girlfriend, but still often felt distant from others except, of course, when drinking. Rather than exploring healthy ways to address these uncomfortable feelings I relied more and more on alcohol to feel less alone.

It has been suggested that a behavior is most likely to be addictive when it serves as the person's primary means to maintain well-being. I understand this to mean a key factor in identifying a substance use disorder is when a person relies on the drug to function and to cope with life's challenges. By the later part of high school this would have been an accurate description of my drinking. Alcohol had become my primary tool in navigating my way through life.

Despite some easily identifiable negative consequences including embarrassing behavior, poor decisions while driving, some nasty hangovers, and occasional black outs, by the end of high school alcohol still seemingly provided more enjoyment than problems in my life. At least that's how I saw it back then. This would certainly change during the next few years while I was in college.

Junior College in California in the early 1980s was almost free. I remember registering for upcoming semesters and the health fee (whatever that was) would be about as much as my classes. The main reason I went to college was because as long as I was in school I could live rent-free at my mom's house. Not exactly the most sincere approach to secondary education, but it made perfect sense at the time.

During the fall of my first year I played baseball for the college's team and still clung to what now had become a far-fetched dream of playing through college and then, maybe, somehow, playing on further. But really, there was no chance I was going to be able to play at that level. By then I was a lot better at drinking than I was at baseball. And honestly, I was a lot more interested in partying than playing.

After about a month of playing fall baseball I quit. I remember walking to my car after telling the coach I was done and thinking, well, now what do I do? What am I now? I was always supposed to be a ballplayer. Who am I now? I couldn't come up with an answer.

Simply stated, the rest of junior college for me was four years (yep, four years to complete two years of study) of wasted time, meaningless relationships, excessive partying, and painfully self-destructive behavior. When you hear people talk about their "college experience" they often speak of meeting new people, making life-long friendships, maybe studying abroad, and, of course, doing some partying. Well, my college experience consisted mostly of dragging my hung-over self to class where I would sit and try to remember what I did the night before.

There was a lot of drug use going on at this time in southern California--a whole lot--and I wasn't missing out on much of it. (I've never seen much benefit in "dru-galogues" [long, detailed descriptions of one's substance use] so I am comfortable with this statement standing on its own.) It wasn't like I was the biggest partier around, but my substance abuse was becoming exceptional.

I remember a college instructor I had for a 7:30 a.m. class asking if he could have a word with me. I waited around after class and he got right to the point, "Have you ever thought about getting help for your drinking?"

Seeing no need to deny what he was suggesting, I just shook my head. He said that although my drinking was not blatantly obvious, as someone personally familiar with alcohol abuse he had on several occasions recognized my condition. He went on to say that he often wondered if I was still drunk from the night before or if I had already been drinking in the morning. I told him it was usually a combination of both. He stated he knew many students drank, and some excessively, but added that none had caught his attention like I had. He suggested I get some help.

I respectfully listened to his comments, agreed I probably drank too much, and thanked him for his concern. I wasn't at all offended. He was right and I didn't deny it one bit. I was twenty years old and on too many mornings I was drunk before most people made it to work. I thought about his words on the way home that day and admitted to myself that I had a problem. Then I went and got hammered drunk--for the next five years.

By the end of college I was no longer drinking to have fun. I was drinking because I had to. I wasn't drinking to cope with life. Drinking was my life. As messed up as I was even I recognized alcohol had completely turned on me. What had seemed to help me in so many ways was no longer working. What used to be my most reliable tool in running my life was now causing me to run out of control. The truth was, as a result of drinking, my life was absolutely imploding physically, mentally, socially, and spiritually.

Years later I came across a saying that went something like alcohol makes everything better until it makes everything worse.

Though I wasn't aware of this saying way back when I was drinking I knew this was happening in my life. The problem was I didn't have any idea what to do about it. And sadly, I had no idea how bad "worse" could get.

While stumbling through college I had managed to do two productive things. The first was earning a degree in Administration of Justice. After having wasted the first two years I saw a counselor who suggested I might want to eventually select a major. I heeded his advice and chose a degree. I made this decision following some less than extensive research which consisted of picking up a course catalog and reading from the beginning of the course offerings. Accounting was listed first, but I had no interest in numbers. Next listed was Administration of Justice. That sounded interesting so the next day I registered for the required courses.

School had always been easy for me (for years I had passed classes without much effort) so even though I continued to drink heavily, I was able to complete all the required courses and actually did quite well. My second accomplishment during college was becoming a good softball player. These two together would get me started in a career that would last for over 30 years.

Receiving the degree put me in a position for some reasonably good employment opportunities, but I actually got a job because of my ability to hit a softball. I had applied for work at a local prison, but after several months still hadn't heard anything. Then one day I learned from a friend that an administrator at the prison wanted me to play on the institution's softball team. Through this friend I was informed that if I would play the prison administrator would hire me. I agreed, went through a rather perfunctory interview and a short time later was hired.

I mention this to illustrate that despite my out of control drinking I still managed to land a decent job, even if not for the most legitimate reasons. Also, the fact that I passed the extensive background investigation required for the job served as an indication of how I had avoided any significant trouble with the law. Although I was falling apart on the inside things still looked okay on the outside.

When I started at the prison the conditions there provided what seemed like perfect excuses for drinking even more. When the job was exciting, finishing a crazy shift gave me a great reason to drink. When it was boring, I told myself I deserved to get drunk. The rotating shifts made associating with friends difficult so, feeling completely justified, I simply started drinking alone much more often. The pay was reasonably good and though I had always found ways to pay for partying it now was even easier to afford.

Over the next couple of years, even though I somehow managed to do well at my job (mostly by becoming more skilled at hiding my drinking and its after-effects) my life went from what was already a steady descent into addiction to an absolute freefall into a personal hell.

As this was happening I withdrew more and more from the people who cared about me. I still spent time with family and friends, but I kept hidden the things that were happening in my life. In the tradition of many addicts before me I utilized an assortment of masks to keep my true self hidden. I had one mask for this group and different masks for other groups. There was one for work, one I wore when around family and another for when I was out at the bar.

The problem was, none of these were the real me. And, unfortunately, in the process of hiding from others I also lost track of who I really was. The one thing I did know was that whoever I was it was probably best if others did not know.

I did an effective job of hiding things from others. In fact, later when I told some of my closest friends I was going to get some help for my drinking they seemed genuinely puzzled by my decision. I had maintained an effective façade that led others to believe I was okay.

But I was not okay. Though the negative consequences to my social life were considerable, the real damage was taking place in my mind, body, and ultimately, my soul. I began to experience what I have seen referred to as addictive thinking, but looking back, a more accurate term may have been distorted or even disturbed thinking. It started with just some irrational reasoning in which I would justify terrible decisions by convincing myself that, really, it made sense to do this or that insane thing. But by the end it included downright bizarre thinking.

Of all the effects drinking had on me, this crazy thinking is probably the hardest to understand. Here's a quick example of how weird it got. At one point, as a result of some health problems, I was being prescribed several medications, all of which came with a warning to avoid alcohol while taking them. Well, there was no way I was going to stop drinking so I didn't take the meds. Yet when asked by the doctor at follow up visits how a particular medication was working I would lie and say it seemed to help. Lying to a doctor is probably not that unusual and may not be considered twisted or bizarre.

What was a little crazy was that when the doctor would prescribe a refill I would go and refill it with no intention of taking the meds. So I ended up with a cabinet full of medication I wasn't taking. I think most people would agree thinking like that was pretty peculiar. But it made sense to me at the time.

The isolation and crazy thinking I was experiencing were tough, but what drove me to my absolute bottom was the damage being done to my body. For years I had experienced severe hangovers which included shaky hands, severe sweating, stomach issues, and generally feeling dreadful. But in the last couple of years the problems went way beyond hangovers. I suffered from problems which often plague heavy drinkers (though not so often 23-year-olds) including signs of liver dysfunction, kidney pain, digestive problems, malnutrition, and several others.

There were two health issues which stood above the rest. The first had to do with my heart. I began to get these intense chest pains, seriously intense. At their worst they would almost take me to the ground. There were many times on the graveyard shift at the prison when I would be walking the hallways and my chest would hurt so bad I would have to stop and lean against the wall.

These events were scary at first (actually, they were terrifying) as I figured I was having a heart attack. But in time I convinced myself it really wasn't that big of a deal. I can't remember what crazy rationale I used, but it must have worked because I continued to party. These "attacks" became so common that several inmates on my assigned housing unit became familiar enough with them to ask me if I was all right on nights when it was obvious I wasn't doing so well.

The second issue was probably the worst of the two. After drinking heavily and partying for a few days I would eventually have to stop because I had to get myself together enough to make it to work. So I would stop using, lose consciousness (often more like passing out than going to sleep), get up for work, and struggle through my shift. The problem was that while I was working my body would start to notice the absence of the alcohol and I would begin to experience withdrawal. By the time I got home I was often in bad shape.

Heroin withdrawal is known to be terribly painful (thankfully, I never experienced that) but alcohol withdrawal is actually more life threatening. In my case it involved unbelievable sweating, my entire body trembling, and rapid irregular heartbeats. Luckily, I didn't experience classic Delirium Tremens (DTs) in that I never had any hallucinations. I did however have seizures or what I called mini-seizures. I had a lot of them.

These episodes, which occurred as I tried to fall asleep, consisted of being jolted off the bed and then shaking violently for just a few seconds. They sometimes got so bad I would lie there, often for up to an hour, just hoping they would stop, one way or another. I don't think I was ever truly suicidal, but many times I was so sick and tired of the seizures that whatever it would have taken to make them stop—to include death—would have been okay with me.

A little over a year before I went to treatment I finally came clean to a doctor about my health. After a couple days of tests (they hooked me up to all kinds of different machines) he told me, in no uncertain terms, my substance abuse was causing severe damage and, left unchecked, would lead to my death. I already knew this, but hearing it from a doctor made it concretely clear.

So I made the last of many futile attempts at sobering up. Mark Twain reportedly once remarked, "Quitting smoking is easy. I've done it a hundred times." That's how it was with my drinking. Over the years I had tried many ways to stop drinking and partying. But each time I failed, usually after only a day or two, and sometimes not even that long.

This time, despite the doctor's warning and all the harm I knew was being done, I failed yet again. Though there was nothing new about it, this particular failure was significant in that it marked the transition in my life when I went from feeling helpless to feeling hopeless. I made the distinction between the two conditions years later while working with other addicts. Briefly, the way I see the difference is that helplessness is when one doesn't believe they can help him or herself. Hopelessness, which is much worse, is when he or she doesn't believe anyone or anything can help them.

Prior to this time I think somewhere in the back of my mind I held out hope that something, someday, might allow me to sober up. But from that point on I really just gave up. I would drink myself into blackouts on my days off, be sick for several days, and then after five or six days of work (with a few drinks throughout to ward off withdrawal), do it all again.

During the last few months of my drinking things got really bad and, honestly, I had pretty much come to terms with the fact my life was coming to an end. I never told this to anyone else. (If I had no other admirable qualities left, at least I wasn't a "poor me" drunk.). I just came to an understanding that this was the deal. I don't ever remember being scared about it. In fact, sometimes when I thought about it, it almost felt like death would be a relief.

In the isolated and selfish life I had created, accepting my plight was not all that difficult. I had seen serious trouble coming for a while and had come to terms with it. It was when I would stop to think about how my situation was affecting others, particularly family members who cared about me, that it became much more complicated.

Of course, this wasn't a problem too often because I

rarely thought about it. People struggling with addiction spend very little time worrying about how they are impacting those who love them. Addicts can't spend too much time on this. It hurts too much. So they just block it out.

I've heard it suggested this blocking out is the result of "denial". The idea is that when denial is at its strongest an addict is actually unable to see how they are hurting others. That may well be true for some addicts, but for me, nothing could be further from the truth.

I was perfectly able to see what was happening, but was unwilling to do so. I purposely avoided thinking about how my addiction and the potentially lethal consequences of it would impact the people who loved me. In fact, whenever these thoughts did come up I drowned them in alcohol. But, despite my best efforts, sometimes reality would break through and force me to look at what was really going on.

One such event that stands out was a day I had gone to visit my sister. I used to love to play with her kids and had been a big part of their lives--particularly her oldest son's. I used to take him with me wherever I went. We would hang around with my friends and many of them considered him one of the guys. He was even the batboy for many of my softball teams. We were more like friends than uncle and nephew; we were buddies.

David was around 11 years old and about the best thing in my life. No matter what condition I was in or what I did he gave me unconditional love. He thought I was the greatest.

On this particular day I remember going to my sister's house and being sick, too sick to hang around and play with David. As I drove home it crossed my mind, matter-of-factly, that I may have seen him for the last time in my life. I loved him and it saddened me to think that I, quite possibly, might never see him again. My heart ached as I thought about this; but not for long. When I got in the house I sat down in a chair and cried.

Then I did what any good drunk does when he comes face-to-face with the damage his drinking is doing to the people he loves the most. I poured a strong drink and then, of course, another.

It's embarrassing to recognize, but when forced to face reality, I was more caught up in how sad I was than in how hurt David might have been had I actually died. As mentioned before, addiction can be an incredibly selfish existence.

I drank for a few more weeks or maybe a couple of months, with the same blackouts, chest pains, seizures, and crazy behavior. And then, finally, one Sunday morning I woke up with a fat lip, a black eye, and very little memory of the entire day before. Nothing completely out of the ordinary in that, but something seemed different this time.

It's difficult to explain, but instead of the awful dread I usually experienced following such a night, I felt a strange kind of relief. It wasn't really a healthy sense of relief, as in this was the last straw and maybe now I could finally straighten up. It was more a relief of surrender, like maybe, one way or another, the end of all this madness was near.

I somehow made it into work that night and ran into a coworker I sometimes talked to during the graveyard shifts. We weren't particularly close, but simply shared the same fate of being bored out of our minds night after night. Most of our previous conversations consisted primarily of meaningless small talk while we killed time.

As I sat down on the other side of his desk, he asked me how I was doing and I knew right away he was asking about more than just the injuries on my face. Though I'm not sure why, I answered him with the truth, the whole truth. I told him my life was crazy and my partying was out of control. He nodded his head knowingly and seemed unfazed by my comments.

I had never talked to this guy about this stuff but he appeared to be very familiar with what I was saying. He listened for a while and then said, "You gotta go to treatment, man. I went and it saved my life." He told me he had been addicted to cocaine and was only able to quit after going to treatment for help.

I had known a few people who had gone to treatment, but I never really considered it a serious option for me. I understood it helped others, but I just didn't ever think it was something I would actually do. We talked for about half an hour and when I told him I was going to get back to work, he suggested one more time, "You really should go to treatment, man."

I stood up from the desk and, surprising even myself, said, "You're right."

Today when I look back at that night, I'm convinced Jesus Christ used that man to reach me. Even though I hadn't asked for help, He knew what I needed. Through my co-worker, Christ was stretching His open arms around me to save me, because it was excruciatingly clear I could not save myself. I simply have no other explanation for what happened.

I went home in the morning and made a difficult phone call to a treatment facility. I picked the phone up and put it back down a couple times, but ultimately, I made the call. I worked the rest of the week (while experiencing some very unpleasant withdrawal symptoms), and then on Friday morning drove myself to a treatment center in a small town in southern California.

I was understandably nervous, but also relieved.

CHAPTER 2

Rescued by Grace

I checked into inpatient treatment in the spring of 1988 arriving, as they say, physically, morally, emotionally, and spiritually bankrupt.

Physically I was a wreck. They took a picture of me when I first arrived at treatment and it clearly showed a sick young man. My face was puffy, my body malnourished, my skin a jaundiced-looking yellow, and my eyes sunken. In addition to the carnage visible in the photo, my hands shook noticeably, my head and body ached, and my stomach was constantly upset.

I felt as if I had completely failed morally. Like many addicts, early in my substance use I had identified certain things that, no matter how much I drank or partied, I would "never" do. And, like many addicts, by the time I got to treatment I had done almost all of them.

I treated people poorly. I lied to and stole from others. I endangered some with aggressive behavior and literally hundreds of others with severely impaired driving. I embarrassed myself, my family and my friends. I spoke and behaved in profane ways which were plainly inexcusable. I had become someone I never wanted to be.

Emotionally I was depressed almost to the point of despair. Because I had drowned my feelings in alcohol for so long I had lost the ability to feel much of anything else. There were two exceptions to this. In addition to feeling depressed, I was still able to feel anger and shame, but that was about it.

I was in no better shape spirituality. I had always believed in God. As a kid I had gone to church with my mom and was even confirmed during junior high. I prayed daily when I was younger and during the years leading up to treatment I had even occasionally prayed for other people. However, even though I didn't doubt God existed and could help others, in those last few years I had come to believe He was no longer a part of my life and as a result I seldom if ever prayed for myself.

There are a number of thoughts about why addicts who once believed in the Lord separate themselves from Him. One is that the addict is angry at God for all the bad things that have happened in his or her life. Another is that the addict, as a result of all the sinful things he or she has done, fears the wrath of God and so tries to hide from Him. Still another is that as the addict slips deeper into addiction God just gets pushed to the side as the addict focuses solely on chasing and using their drug of choice.

While all of these explanations likely played some part in my situation, none explained it completely. I didn't necessarily fear or blame God, nor did I forget Him. I just got to the point where I felt unworthy to turn to Him. I felt like He had done His part and I had let Him down by destroying the life he had given me. I had heard when I was younger that our bodies were God's temple. Well, I felt terrible about what I had done to that temple. I was ashamed to face God and so I had drifted from Him.

So I showed up at the front door of the treatment facility in bad shape. In short, I was broken and lost.

The program was 28-days long and based on the 12-Steps of Alcoholics Anonymous (AA) and the disease module of addiction. It featured a holistic approach to treatment which meant we addressed all facets of life. We exercised and ate nutritious meals to improve our physical health, and we attended lectures to increase our knowledge of addiction as a disease. We participated in groups where we addressed emotional issues and worked with each other to develop better relationship skills. We discussed spirituality and had days when we addressed family issues. We were even assigned daily chores to improve personal responsibility and practice caring for others.

Following my initial check-in, which included a medical evaluation, the staff immediately gave me some medication and put me to bed. I had not had a drink for five days and I was still experiencing severe withdrawal symptoms. They told me the medication would help with the withdrawal and get me settled down enough to benefit from treatment activities.

Though I was knocked out for much of the first three days, there were periods of consciousness when I just lay in my bed and stared at the ceiling. I felt terribly ashamed for being there and berated myself for being so screwed up. But something else was happening. I couldn't help but think there must be a reason for me being there. I just couldn't believe that I, of my own accord, could have done something as responsible as getting help.

The thing that kept coming to mind was maybe God wanted me there.

Earlier in my life I believed God had a plan for all of us, but because I had been distant from Him for so long I didn't really consider that idea as being relevant to my life anymore. Yet as I ran over and over through my mind all that was happening to me I could come up with only one explanation. I believed God must have brought me there.

On Monday the staff determined I was stable enough to begin programming. Almost immediately, I realized participating in group activities posed a bigger problem for me than did the physical withdrawal for which they had initially treated me. I was used to feeling sick after partying heavily for a few days. I could handle withdrawal pretty well. What I was not at all used to was interacting with other people and I was especially uncomfortable talking about my feelings with these people.

During the last several years of my drinking my relationships had become more and more superficial. I had family I loved and people I cared about, but there was no one, other than maybe my oldest sister, with whom I had shared anything of any real significance. It seemed as my addiction progressed I trusted people less and less.

The sad thing was, during the same time, I began to trust alcohol, the thing that was destroying my life, more and more. As my isolation increased I also came to believe I needed people less and less and, of course, I needed alcohol more and more.

This way of thinking was hardly unique to me. Many active alcoholics will tell you that despite the damage caused by their drinking they still believe with all their heart the thing they need more than anything else is another drink.

In the movie *My Name Is Bill W*, James Woods stars as the title character who was a co-founder of AA. There's a scene in which he is talking to his wife about his wildly out of control drinking. He explains to her how alcohol has turned on him and describes all the harm his drinking has caused, including how he has given up on himself and even given up on God. He tells her about the incredible guilt he feels and how terrible he feels about what he has done to her.

He then walks toward her, looks her in the eyes and says that despite all this carnage and heartache what he wants right at that minute, more than anything else, is another drink. When I saw the movie a few years after treatment I completely understood his way of thinking.

Now, sober and in a treatment facility, I was going to have to learn how to deal with people again. And because I had failed to develop many basic social skills as an adolescent I would essentially be starting from scratch.

Right from the first group meeting interacting with the others was a struggle. Making the situation even more difficult was the frequency and intensity of these interactions. In addition to group sessions during the day, we also got up early every morning and exercised together, ate together three times a day, went to support groups every night, and then slept in two-person rooms.

This schedule left virtually no opportunity for hiding, physically or emotionally, from others. After years of living alone (at least emotionally) I was suddenly spending my entire day participating in exhaustive interactions with people I didn't even know.

After only a couple of days the counselors recognized I was struggling so they pulled me in for a meeting. They politely but firmly informed me I would have to learn to work with other group members if I was to benefit from treatment. I left the meeting feeling angry and a little overwhelmed. I went to my room and for the first time in a while I prayed to God and this time I asked Him to help me.

Beginning with my very first meeting at the facility we had prayed the Serenity Prayer and the Lord's Prayer at the end of each session. I had known both of these prayers for years, but had never actually considered how they might apply directly to my life. I had prayed them more through rote memorization than with any real awareness of what they actually meant.

But now, as I sat in the hospital praying, for the first time I clearly understood the Serenity Prayer. I prayed it earnestly and asked God for the courage to deal with these people around whom I felt so foreign. I can't say I was immediately transformed, but in the next couple of days, as I continued to pray for strength to get involved in the program, I was able to begin meaningful communication with my peers.

In the following days, as I participated more and more in treatment activities, I believed my prayers were being answered.

I began to benefit from the interaction with my peers and the counselors, and as I did I saw it as another indication God was helping me out of the mess I had made of my life.

During the first couple of weeks I was introduced to the 12 Steps of Alcoholics Anonymous (AA) with particular emphasis on the first three steps. Many addicts struggle with this part of the program because they must admit powerlessness over their addiction, acknowledge that a higher power could help them regain control, and turn their lives over to this higher power.

For me the first part of the program was not at all difficult. My life was so obviously unmanageable it was actually a relief to finally be able to just say out loud, "My life is crazily out of control."

The second part, believing God could and would help me, was not quite as easy. As I mentioned earlier, I had never stopped believing in God but, sitting there in treatment, I felt so ashamed of myself I didn't believe I deserved any help or blessings from Him. This shame, which was labeled self-loathing by treatment staff, proved to be a major obstacle in the initial stage of treatment.

An event early in treatment provided some insight into just how damaged my self-concept was. During the first week I was given the Minnesota Multiphasic Personality Inventory (MMPI), a lengthy questionnaire used to assess personality traits and mental illness.

A few days later the program psychiatrist, with whom I had met once before the test, called me into his office. He said I would have to take the test again because my scores indicated such extreme "self-loathing" that, if taken to be legitimate, he would have to take action to prevent me from self-harm.

The doctor stated that he did not think I was as bad off as the test indicated, but rather that my anger (toward myself) and shame had so influenced my answers that the test was invalid. He suggested we wait awhile (to give me time to settle down emotionally) and then test again. About a week later I took the test again and the doctor said that although the results still showed high levels of shame and anger, the scores were much closer to being within normal limits.

As I got more deeply involved in group sessions my issues with shame also became apparent to staff and other group members. In order to work through this I was encouraged to explore the origin of such feelings. My counselors and peers suggested it was a result of my childhood and the fact I grew up around alcoholism. They said I was feeling shame based on the actions of others and how they made me feel.

Though I understood this concept and even accepted it to a degree, while honestly exploring my past I had discovered the shame I felt was based mostly on my own actions. I, like many addicts, grew up saying I would never be like the alcoholics I knew as a child. Sitting in those groups, examining my life, I came to the painful realization that not only had I become just like them, I was even worse.

This failure to avoid becoming like other addicts was the driving force behind my shame.

While looking back at my past, I also recognized there were times when I felt ashamed of my drinking even while actively getting drunk. I'm not talking about embarrassing incidents, of which I had a seemingly endless number. I understood such stupid behavior was just part of drinking too much. Rather, the moments that stuck out were the times when I had stopped and really looked at my life--not what I was doing, but who I was becoming.

One incident I remembered was in a little bar in a Chinese restaurant. It was early afternoon and I was already very drunk. I went to the restroom in the back just like I had a thousand times before, but this time as I staggered by the sink I caught a glimpse of my reflection in the mirror. I tried to laugh off the first sight of my drunkenness, but a second, more reality-based examination revealed that there was nothing funny about the person in that mirror.

I stood in front of the mirror for a minute and felt this incredible shame at what I saw: a stumbling drunk young man who, in the middle of a workday, had absolutely no other plans for the day (or the next) except to get even drunker. I experienced a sinking feeling in my gut and then had what might be called a moment of clarity. I specifically remember thinking, what happened? I was supposed to be somebody.

The thing was, early in life, my family and other people often told me I would amount to something. I had been in a program for mentally gifted kids during elementary school, was a leader among my peers, and was always a pretty good athlete. So it seemed I had a lot of potential.

I realized right there in front of that mirror I wasn't doing much with my potential. I remember walking back through the restaurant feeling worthless.

But as I rounded the corner and approached the bar I decided exactly what I needed to do. I sat down and purposely drank as fast as I could to rid myself of the worthless feeling. Although I don't remember specifically, there is a good chance before that night was over I behaved in ways which ultimately led to even more shame.

I had several of these moments of clarity in the last few years of drinking, but I was never able to take any constructive action when they occurred. Instead, this self-destructive cycle, drinking to drown my feelings of shame and by doing so creating more shame, drove me deeper and deeper into my addiction.

So there I was about a week into treatment--stuck. Though I had easily accepted and completed the first Step; admitting my life was unmanageable, I was unable to proceed any further. It was obvious shame was keeping me from Step Two; believing God could and would restore me. I didn't believe I was worthy of being restored. Which meant I wouldn't be able to practice the most important of the first three Steps; turning my life over to God.

I had identified the problem: shame. I just didn't know what to do about it. The one thing I did know was blaming it on others was not going to help. I was ashamed of me and not anybody else.

In hindsight it seems clear what I needed more than anything was a restoration of my relationship with God. My shame wasn't based so much on my relationships with other people. It was based on my relationship with God. And until I got right with Him I would not be able to make any meaningful progress in recovery. What I needed right then was someone who could lead me back toward Christ.

Thankfully, God provided that someone in the form of my counselor. Though we worked with all treatment staff we were each assigned one primary counselor. The one to whom I was assigned couldn't have been a better match for me. She was a recovering woman who had previously been a nun. She had a thorough understanding of spirituality and the importance of faith.

What was most important was that my counselor had first-hand knowledge and real-life experience in what it felt like to have let God down.

While compassionately sharing her wisdom she told me no matter what any of us had done forgiveness was available through the sacrifice of Jesus Christ. All we had to do was confess our sins, ask for forgiveness, and accept Him as our Lord and Savior. I responded by saying I knew about Christ, but didn't think He could forgive me for how I had wasted the gifts I'd been given.

My counselor gently informed me that people much worse than I had been saved. What she was saying was hard for me to accept, but when she shared some of the mistakes she had made in her life I began to experience a little hope. I thought that if after all she'd been through she could feel secure in the forgiveness of Christ, maybe I could do the same.

The work I did with my counselor was easily the most

significant part of my treatment. She helped me understand God loved me and my forgiveness and salvation were not contingent on what I had done, but rather on what Christ had done on the cross for me. My being saved would not be based on how bad I was or was not, but on Christ dying to save me from my sins.

She helped me see that God would forgive me if I would accept His grace through faith in Jesus Christ as my savior. She didn't preach at me. She simply shared the Good News with me in a caring way.

My counselor was literally a Godsend and her guidance was the key to breaking through the shame that had me stuck. I didn't magically start feeling great about myself, but I was able to go from feelings of abject worthlessness to believing that, despite all I had done, I had worth simply because God loved me.

I still recall her writing in my daily journal these very words, "Remember you are loved." Reading these words, and for the first time in a long time truly believing them, allowed me to complete the second and third Steps. I came to believe Jesus Christ, a power greater than myself, could lead me to sanity and that I was ready to turn my life over to Him.

That is what I did, and He saved my life.

I continued to participate in all aspects of treatment, but really, after I was able to consciously turn my life over to Christ my recovery became less about learning new life skills and more about trusting God to direct my steps. I began to read the Bible and took time to contemplate what the Gospel really meant to me. I found enlightening verses almost every time I picked up my Bible.

For the first time I read Philippians 4:13, "I can do all things through Christ who strengthens me", and believed it was true for me. In the past I had tried so many times to change my life and each time had failed miserably. These words helped me see I didn't have to try to change my life on my own; I could rely on

Christ for strength to meet the many challenges of recovery.

I also began to pray more intently than I had ever prayed before. Each time I did so I asked, "God please help me stay clean and sober, and please help me turn to You for strength." I prayed this prayer over and over several times per day. As the days passed I began to feel truly strengthened through the Lord.

These words, as much as anything in treatment, moved me toward the thing I needed most in my life; hope. And once I gained a sense of hope my entire outlook on life changed.

One of my clearest memories of treatment is of a day my mom and sister came to visit me. Our previous visits had been meaningful and helpful, but really kind of depressing because each involved looking at the mess I had made of my life. This day was different.

During a break we went outside to shoot baskets around an old hoop and decided to play a game of H O R S E. But, as I tossed the basketball to my mom so she could go first I suggested we spell out H O P E instead of H O R S E.

I know how corny this sounds, but if you could have been there and experienced the relief we all felt you'd understand the significance. Their son and littlest brother was sick and had nearly died. Now, standing around a silly old basketball hoop, I had at long last expressed a sense of hope.

The life skills learned in treatment were helpful, as was the support of my family and peers, but nothing compared to this life-changing, life-saving sense of hope I gained by turning my life over to Jesus Christ.

Years after treatment I heard someone once describe addicts as having a God-shaped hole in their heart (likely taken from Pascal's quote: "There is a God shaped vacuum in the heart of every man which cannot be filled by any created thing, but only by God . . . ").

The way I understood this was that people who become addicts have within themselves a hole or an empty place. In the course of developing and maintaining their addiction they try all kinds of different ways to fill this void, including alcohol, drugs, sex, money, power, or whatever they think might work.

The problem is that despite the addict's best efforts to make these work (and some keep trying for years and years, at great cost) none of them fit exactly into the painful empty spot in their life. It's like trying a wrong piece in a puzzle. You want it to fit, you try to force it to fit, but try as you might it's just not going to work.

While in treatment I recognized I had spent years trying to fill a huge hole in my soul. I'd tried all the usual things people try and they had all left me hurting. When I finally stopped chasing worldly solutions to my pain and decided to give my life to Christ I began to feel complete. Though I wasn't familiar with this terminology at the time, I had discovered the gaping hole in my soul was indeed God-shaped.

After 28 days I was ready to leave treatment. I would leave believing my life could be different. I came in feeling worthless, but now possessed a budding sense of worth and belonging gained from the understanding of God's love for me. I arrived consumed by hopelessness, but would be leaving with a belief that, with God's help, I could live a meaningful life.

Where I was once just waiting to die, I now believed I had purpose and I could do something with my life.

This concept came clearly into focus on one of my last days in treatment when I remembered a brief conversation I had years earlier with my junior high counselor. He had approached me as I was lounging around the library while my classmates were studying and out of the blue asked me, "What do want to do with your life?"

I sarcastically replied, "I think I'll be the president of the United States."

Unimpressed and unperturbed by my smart aleck response, he proceeded to answer his own question, "You know, you can be whatever you want to be." He finished his brief comments be emphatically stating, "You don't have to be just another partier Rich. You can do something with your life."

I pretended to laugh off his comments and left the building. But his words were on my mind as I walked home that day. Here was a guy who knew what I was involved in and how I was living (it was really no secret, the way I dressed and the people I hung around with gave anyone familiar with teenagers a good idea of what I was up to), and yet he was telling me I could be whatever I wanted to be; that I could be somebody.

Though it had been many years, as I sat there at the treatment facility, I could still vividly remember walking home that day and how much I wished I could believe what he had said. But the sad truth was, by eighth grade I was already defining myself as a partier or stoner and, other than a baseball player, not much else. In subsequent years his words and the idea I could do something meaningful in life were gradually washed away by waves of alcohol and reckless living.

But now, as I prepared to start my life over, his words had returned. And for the first time in a long time, maybe the first time ever, I believed them.

I had arrived at treatment broken and lost. I left with hope and a strong belief I could be made whole through Christ who strengthened me. I left believing I had been found and that Jesus Christ had saved my life. And I left believing that He had a plan for my life, that I had been rescued for a reason.

CHAPTER 3

Following Christ Through Adversity

W hen I got home from treatment there was no parade, banners, ticker tape, nor marching bands. People hadn't all quit drinking, they hadn't boarded up all the bars in town, and drug use had not been eliminated. In fact, things were exactly as they were when I left a month earlier.

After spending time in treatment where all daily events are built around recovery and almost everyone encountered is concerned with and supportive of recovery, it can be quite challenging for a person to return to the real world. If they haven't been forewarned they are often surprised to find that although they have changed the way they think, changed the way they behave, and even changed what they believe, things in the real world have not changed at all.

I was fortunate enough to have been warned about this reality by my counselors. It was a good thing too, because I found out immediately that just as they had suggested, nothing had changed. Everyone I knew was doing exactly what they were doing when I left. Everything in the community, the bars, drinking, partying, drugs, and crazy behavior, was also the same as before.

I figured out right away if my life was going to change for the better it was going to take some hard work. I was going to

have to try completely new ways of living, because my old environment was certainly not going to be magically transformed to
fit my new lifestyle.

I was okay with this. I left treatment with a firm understanding that although I had turned my life over to Christ, sobriety was not going to be easy.

My brother, who was in recovery, helped me understand
this by telling me, "With faith you can move a mountain, but
you've got to bring a shovel." I memorized this phrase and used it
often to remind me that while faith was to be the cornerstone of
my sobriety I would still need to do the daily work of recovery.
I accepted this as fact and began to develop a strong belief that
as long as I continued to trust God and worked hard at recovery I
could be successful.

One of the first things I did was establish a daily routine
which included work, exercise, healthy meals, and lots of reading.
I decided to be like a sponge and soak up all the literature I could.
I continued to read the Bible and added several daily meditation
books. This reading proved to be of great benefit and my faith
grew stronger as I got deeper into God's word. To this day I still encourage those leaving treatment to make time to read.

In addition to the literature I also benefited from being
open-minded toward the people who continued to come into my
life. During treatment it had been suggested that if I trusted the
Lord, He would provide timely help. This certainly turned out to
be true for me when it came to encountering the right people at
the right time. Just like the coworker who encouraged me to go to
treatment and my counselor while there, when I started to seek
spiritual growth and understanding, help seemed to come from
all kinds of different people in all kinds of unexpected places.

Early on I was helped by a small group of people at work
with whom I had never previously discussed matters of faith.
When I mentioned to one of them that I was trying to develop

a stronger relationship with God, they all eagerly offered to help and shared with me many valuable insights about their own faith. Ultimately my beliefs did not completely align with theirs, but I've always been grateful for their help in those early days.

I was also helped by two men who I'd worked with for years. I knew they were both Christians but had never related to them on that level. However, when I returned to work they both stepped up and helped guide me along my path by sharing spiritual wisdom and providing positive role models of healthy Christian men.

I read several years later that Confucius once said, "When the student is ready the teacher will appear." I knew he wasn't talking about Christianity, but when I came across the quote I thought, that's what happened to me. Whenever I prepared myself to learn, it just happened a teacher always came along.

I believed then, as I do now, these people were put into my life by God. This was especially true for encounters which occurred away from the prison. These encounters involved people who seemingly came out of the blue to provide meaningful spiritual guidance and were some of the most enlightening experiences in my early recovery.

Two particular instances stand out above the rest. The first occurred at 6:30 one morning as I stood alone in a nearly abandoned industrial park. I had been dropped off and was waiting for a shop owner who had repaired my car.

Standing in the dimly lit parking lot, I saw a man moving through the morning fog directly toward me. He walked right up to me and said good morning. After some very brief small talk he said, "So, you're in recovery."

I just smiled, shook his hand and said, "You know what man, I am." It's funny but I never really gave much thought to how he would know. It just seemed to make sense that he did.

For about the next 15 minutes this guy shared some awesome words about his belief in God and how his faith had changed his life. He told me his life had gotten so completely out of control that he was about ready to give up. He said when he was at his lowest point, in desperation he reached out to God and was saved.

He went on to say that once he had accepted Christ his life was never the same. When the shop opened I told him I needed to get my car, shook his hand again, and thanked him for sharing with me. When I came out of the shop he was gone.

The second encounter happened one afternoon on a basketball court. All the other guys had left but I was shooting around a little by myself. As I was finishing up this older man walked up to the court. He said hello and asked me a few things about basketball and then suddenly asked, "Do you know Jesus Christ? Do you have a personal relationship with Him?"

Just like in the parking lot I smiled and said, "You know what, man? Yes, I do."

For the next 30 minutes we talked about Christ and His love for us. He told me no matter what I had done God still loved me. When I told him I had to get going he provided me with some words of encouragement and even recommended several Bible verses.

People crossing my path like this helped my faith continue to grow, and as my faith grew, the hope born in treatment also increased. I started to really believe things could get better and it seemed like events in my life began to fit together as if part of a design.

For instance, prior to treatment I made it a habit to purposely avoid or ignore other people, particularly those I didn't know. If I hadn't learned in treatment to interact with others I would have simply ignored these two people and others who gave me help early in my journey. I thought about this often and came to believe this "design" was the work of the Lord.

Rekindled was the belief I had as a kid that God had a plan for all of us. I was already fairly sure this explained what was happening in my life, but after a particular event about two and a half months after treatment, I became absolutely certain of it.

It happened one Friday night when a friend and I were at home getting ready to watch an L.A. Lakers playoff game. Just before game time some friends called and invited me down to a pizza place to watch the game. I knew there would be lots of drinking so I politely declined.

At the same time a young woman was invited by one of her friends to the same game at the same restaurant, but she too initially declined.

My friend and I watched the first part of the game and then at halftime I suddenly said, "Let's go down to Rusty's."

He said something like, "I thought you didn't want to go down there."

To which I replied, "Well, I do now."

He wasn't sure what was going on and truthfully, I wasn't either. I just knew I needed to go. Across town, the aforementioned woman also had a change of heart and decided to go meet her friends and watch the game. She would later recall she wasn't sure what made her change her mind, she just felt like she should go.

My friend and I got there, ordered a couple of cokes and sat down. Because we were the only two not drinking I felt awkward and even thought about leaving. But for some reason I didn't and the rest, as they say, is history.

About ten minutes later, the same young lady arrived to meet with her friends and the moment I saw her I knew I had to meet her. We ended up sitting in her car and talking until 3:30 in the morning that night. I knew my life would never be the same.

Meeting Tracy was simply the greatest thing God has ever done for me, far greater than anything I ever deserved. I was blessed beyond anything I had ever imagined that night. We were married and I have loved her every day for over 30 years.

More than any other person, Tracy has helped me grow spiritually. She has supported me in every one of my efforts to help other addicts, and by always believing in me, she has given me hope. Of all the people the Lord put into my life none impacted me the way my wife has. She ended years of painful isolation and opened the way for me to do the most important work of my life; loving my children.

We have two daughters (and four grandkids) and if you think I get sentimental talking about my wife, well, I won't even try to tell you how I feel about these incredible gifts from God. Though our girls are grown I am still easily the proudest dad (and granddad) in the world. I just don't have the words to describe how much I love these children. So as Forest Gump would say, "That's all I have to say about that."

As my faith grew, it affected my life in some unexpected ways. One of the more interesting was its impact on my participation in 12-Step groups. I had attended an AA or NA (Narcotics Anonymous) meeting every night while in treatment and benefited greatly from the experience. When I left treatment I was encouraged to do the standard 90 meetings in 90 days.

I didn't come close. About six weeks out, after attending fewer and fewer group meetings each week, I stopped going to meetings (though I did continue to read AA literature for a couple years).

Alcoholics Anonymous is helpful for many recovering people. It definitely helped me early on and I have referred literally hundreds of people to this program. However, for some people, the spiritual part is problematic. This was true for me, though not in the usual way.

Many individuals who struggle with AA are put off by the "God thing." They are uncomfortable being encouraged to find a Higher Power because to them it feels like they are being told that they have to believe in God in order to work the steps and benefit from the program.

My problem was not that I was pushed to believe in God. My issue was that as I worked to turn my life over to the Lord, specifically Jesus Christ, I struggled with the ambiguity inherent in the idea of a Higher Power. Many times during meetings I felt uncomfortable when listening to people speaking in vague terms about their Higher Power.

I never begrudged anyone their beliefs, but for me the vagueness was very disconcerting. I soon came to the conclusion that faith in Christ was the foundation of my recovery, and as such, I needed to stay focused solely on Christianity. I knew the concept of a Higher Power worked for many, but I recognized it wasn't helping me. So I stopped attending 12-step meetings.

During the next few months I worked on turning my life completely over to Christ. This involved listening for His call and living according to His will for me. But even as I tried to do the right thing each day, there were still serious challenges early on. Two of the most significant challenges were cravings to drink and boredom. On several occasions, when I experienced these two simultaneously, it seemed like I was about to go crazy.

Probably the worst time was a day off during the week when I decided to go by myself to see a movie. I was sitting in the theater feeling extremely bored and decided to get some candy (many recovering drinkers crave sugar and I was no exception). As I walked out toward the concessions all of the sudden, out of nowhere I had the powerful, matter-of-fact thought, I'm going to go get a drink.

My heart started to race and I kind of panicked. I could even feel a sort of pre-using buzz as my brain began to anticipate a shot of alcohol. (This is also common among addicts and many in treatment report that while using they would get a buzz just from knowing they were about to drink or use.)

I looked around for help or maybe a useful distraction, but being a weekday it was only me and the kid at the concession counter. I didn't think he would be very interested in, or of much help with, my predicament. I stepped into the bathroom and stopped right in the middle of the room. I stood there perplexed and experienced the frightening realization that I was not going to be able to handle this craving.

Faced with what seemed like inevitable relapse, I did something I had never done in all the times I tried to quit drinking. I folded my hands, bowed my head and prayed something like, "God, please help me through this. I don't think I can do this alone. I want to believe I can do all things through the strength you give me. Please God, help me stay sober."

Totally forgetting about the movie (cravings can be incredibly powerful) I walked outside, got into my car, and prayed another quick prayer asking Christ for help. I drove out onto the freeway and headed in the direction of a particular bar I was familiar with down by the beach in Ventura. As I approached the freeway exit that would take me to the bar I really wasn't sure which way I would go.

By the grace of God and the strength He provided, I kept driving. I headed further north and parked right next to the beach. I got out and let the afternoon breeze push past me. For a guy who'd been panicking just minutes before I felt amazingly well. It had been a close call, but with Divine assistance I had made it through. When I was getting back into my car to leave I took a minute and thanked God. Then I drove home--sober.

This incident and several others like it confirmed what I had discovered during a month of self-examination while in treatment: I wasn't very good at running my life. Left to my own devises I had a powerful propensity to get drunk. There was no getting around that fact.

However, in the first few months following treatment I had also recognized that when I trusted God to guide me I was able to stay on track in moving my life in a new direction. That is, as long as I did my part and remained committed to the daily work of recovery.

Over the next few months I focused primarily on two concepts: one, I couldn't run my life very well but Christ could, and two, I needed to do the footwork of recovery. I combined the two and came up with a philosophy: trust God and work hard. I adopted it as my slogan for living.

To help me visualize this, I used an analogy many have used in recovery. I thought of it like a tandem bicycle with me in the back peddling and Christ up front doing the steering. I'd learned I wasn't a good driver, but I believed I could be a darn good peddler. Together I believed we could make a good team.

This is how I began to approach each day, praying for strength to do what was required and faith to trust God to steer me in the direction He wanted my life to go.

During the next year and a half, my life did become more meaningful. I was married, started a family, and even my work at the prison was going well. I continued to read and pray daily and we joined a local church. There were, of course, challenges along the way, but by working with Tracy and relying on God for strength I managed to get through them, often feeling stronger on the other side of the adversity.

Then about two years into recovery something troubling began to happen. I started to feel <u>bored</u>. Not in the crazy restless way I use to, but rather a feeling like there was supposed to be something more to this recovery thing. I kicked the idea around for a month or two and then decided to mention it to a guy at work who was also in recovery.

Although we weren't close friends he had been the first one to visit me at treatment. He was familiar with the treatment facility and was able to get in while I was still in detox. He came and sat with me when I was just getting off of the medication and though I barely remembered it I always appreciated his visit.

One day at work I mentioned to him I was feeling bored and he asked, "How long have you been sober?"

I told him about two years and practically before I finished speaking he said, "You're ready to start serving others."

I asked for some clarification about what he meant and he quickly explained that lots of recovering people, at about two years of sobriety, begin to feel a need to start giving back to the program (as he referred to his 12-Step recovery). Other than a couple brief conversations during softball tournaments, I had hardly talked to this man since returning to work.

Yet he summed up my situation like he knew exactly what I was going through. He provided me with just what I needed to hear at that moment and interestingly, I never again talked to him about sobriety.

I considered my friend's advice and it seemed to make sense. In addition to believing that God had a general plan for my life, ever since treatment I had also thought I'd been saved for a specific reason. I was now thinking helping others just might be this special purpose. But I also knew following his suggestion would pose a significant challenge.

One of the main characteristics of my addiction was I had isolated myself and pulled away from other people. As I mentioned earlier, during the last couple years of my drinking, I pretty much existed alone. I didn't want anyone involved in the mess my life had become and I wasn't much interested in others people's issues either. So this serving others thing was not going to be easy.

The first thing I did was discuss this idea with my wife Tracy and we decided I should begin to pray for guidance. I tried several different prayers and finally settled on one I said daily for the better part of the next decade. My simple prayer was this, "God, please put me in a position where I can help others." I'm convinced this dozen-word prayer helped shape the rest of my life.

I began to explore different ways of helping others and initially didn't have much luck. I went to my old junior high school and asked my counselor (the same man mentioned earlier) if I could speak to students about drug abuse. He said that because of legal issues I could not.

I considered maybe doing something for the church, but honestly, I didn't feel completely comfortable there. I thought about speaking at AA or NA meetings, but since I wasn't involved in the program any longer that didn't seem practical either.

Then one day I walked into one of the living units at work and saw a piece of paper on the staff desk. I picked it up and found it contained information about a certificate program at a local junior college for drug abuse counseling. I made a copy of the paper, took it with me, and on the next available registration date I signed up for the program.

As I prepared for the classes to start, I realized God had begun to answer my prayers. I truly believed He was getting me ready to help others.

The certificate program would take two years, so in the meantime I decided to try to serve others through my job, which at the time involved work with both male and female inmates. Though I knew this wouldn't be easy in my position as a guard, I began to do my best by treating inmates with compassion and, when possible, talking to them in encouraging ways.

There were several inmates with whom I had some good conversations and with a few I even developed an ongoing rapport. However, despite my effort it soon seemed clear prison would not be the place where I would fulfill my calling. Though the institution I worked at wasn't particularly harsh, (in fact it was downright pleasant by California standards) it was still a toxic environment and day after day I came across inmates who made it very difficult for me to want to help them or anyone else.

After several months in which I experienced very limited success, one particular incident effectively ended my attempt to serve others; at least others who were in prison. I was working the front lobby during inmate visiting and I saw a woman walking toward the front door with a little kid who appeared to be wearing a ski mask. Considering that we were in southern California this, of course, caught my attention.

As the woman and the boy entered the building, I looked

out through the glass separating me from the visitors and saw one of the most disturbing things I'd ever seen.

This little boy's entire head had been horribly burned and disfigured. Seeing him as he stood there I recalled hearing other officers speaking about a new female inmate who, while high on drugs, had (this is difficult to write) submerged her child in boiling water. I put the two together and realized this was the child they had been talking about.

While I was checking the woman's ID I learned the little boy was in fact there to see his mother. I then noticed the boy was looking up through the glass at me, so I looked down and, trying to be nice, smiled at him. He smiled back and it was only then that I saw the full extent of his injuries. This five- or six-year-old boy, just a little kid, had no face. Gone were his nose, lips, and ears.

My heart hurt for him as bad as anything I think I'd ever felt. I was heart-sick and furious at the same time. He went into the visiting room and I went about the business of completing my shift.

Driving home that day I did two things. First, I cried for that little boy (all these years later it still deeply grieves me). The second thing I did was decide I was done with trying to help others, particularly female inmates. How could I be compassionate toward people who could do such terrible things; especially after encountering a woman who could do something like this to her own child?

I decided I was done caring for anyone at the prison. It simply hurt too much to be caring in such a cruel environment. In all the years I had spent being disconnected from others I had never felt pain like I felt that day. If this was what being compassionate got a person, I decided I'd had my fill.

So, from that point on, as far as I was concerned how an inmate felt or what they needed was none of my concern. I implemented a strategy to simply do my job and disregard the emotional component of daily prison life. With amazing speed I perfected this technique. Just a month or two later, after watching me coldly handle a situation with an injured and distraught inmate, a coworker derisively referred to me as a robot. I took it as a complement.

For the next two years I experienced a powerful struggle in my life. After having been blessed with significant progress in my war between drinking and sobriety, I now faced another battle between two conflicting forces. Some people refer to this struggle as the worldly versus the Godly, others term it the human versus spiritual, and still others call it good versus evil.

Whatever this struggle was called, it felt like I was being pulled in two different directions right at the time when I thought my purpose in life was beginning to come into focus.

On the one hand I was attending college and trying to follow God's call to serve others. On the other, circumstances at work were pushing away from wanting to help anyone else.

The most trying of these circumstances was physical altercations with inmates. I was never involved in any outrageous incidents like the ones shown in the media, but I was involved in a good number of ugly altercations. I was injured a few times and on more than a few occasions returned the favor and injured inmates. As these and other negative experiences accumulated I went from trying to help the inmates, to being purposefully indifferent toward them, to actually hating them.

Two particular events brought this conflict between my spiritual calling and worldly forces to the brink. The first occurred in the hospital at the prison. I was sometimes tasked with taking photographs of assault victims and on this particular day a guy had been severely injured by another inmate. He had been hit in the face with a dumb bell while lying on his back bench-pressing weights.

I walked into the nurse's station as she was getting ready to treat him and told her to wait until I could get some good shots of his injuries. She said he was badly hurt and needed immediate treatment. I said something to the effect of, "Look, as soon as I get the photos, I don't care what you do with him."

She glared at me and with utter disdain said, "What's wrong with you? How could you say such a thing?"

I kind of blew it off at the time, but a while later I thought, man, that was messed up for me to act like that.

The other event happened during the L.A. riots. While driving home from school the first night of the disturbance I had been listening to all the craziness on the radio and pulled into the garage feeling furious about what was happening. As I got out of the car my wife stepped into the garage and I just exploded saying some awful things about the people involved in the riots.

Tracy was clearly upset (really, I think she was hurt more than anything else) and said she had never heard me talk like that before. She was right. I had never talked like that around her and certainly never like that around my home. After she went to bed I sat and thought about what I had said, what she had said, and how I had affected her. I knew I was becoming someone I didn't want to be.

Though I had continued praying that God would put me in a position to help others and was even taking practical steps to make it happen, I was simultaneously being made bitter and mean by the world. Eventually, it became unavoidably clear I could not pursue both God's plan for my life and continue to work at the prison.

Realizing this, my wife and I knew we had to make some hard decisions. Leaving my job seemed like the obvious thing to do as far as my spiritual health, but it would create serious financial hardships for us. Staying at the prison made sense economically, but it also had the potential of virtually destroying me spiritually.

We talked and prayed about this difficult situation for several weeks and ultimately decided not only would I leave the prison, but we would leave the state. We believed God had a plan for us and didn't think we could effectively follow it if I remained at the prison or if we remained in California. In our hearts we believed we were being called to make a fresh start.

So the day after I received my counseling certificate from the college we moved to the Minnesota. We had no employment lined up, but we were sure if we trusted God and were willing to work hard good things would happen.

Five years into my recovery I had been forced to decide whether to pursue a life shaped by the will of Jesus Christ or to have my life molded by the world. With the help of my wife I decided to follow Christ.

CHAPTER 4

Persevering to Blessings

I n the first few months following our move I learned making a commitment to follow Christ didn't guarantee life would go exactly the way I thought it would. I also discovered believing God had a plan for me and knowing what the plan was were two different things. I soon realized just how strong my faith would need to be if I was to continue following His will.

I left California with the goal of finding a job helping people overcome addiction. My attempts to help at the prison had failed miserably and left me bitter toward the inmates. I now hoped to work with "regular" people who were not so deeply involved with the legal system or the criminal lifestyle. That's what I thought I was supposed to do, but it didn't quite work out that way.

When I began looking for employment I couldn't find any opportunity to do substance abuse counseling. In fact, I had no luck finding any work at all. After several weeks of this I started to have some doubts about my decision to leave the good job I had back home.

However, I kept looking and a couple of months later found work at a group home for youth. This position had potential, but it wasn't a good fit. It just didn't feel right to me. Maybe the transition from prison guard to youth worker was too big of a switch or maybe this just wasn't my calling. Either way, I only worked there for a few months.

While working at the group home I met a man who worked for the state. After learning of my background he helped me get a side job writing Pre-Sentence Investigations (PSI) for the courts. After doing just several of these I was hired as a full-time, but temporary, probation officer. This position paid well and I really didn't mind working with people who were in trouble (most of it was minor stuff), but once again, I couldn't help but think this wasn't what I was supposed to be doing.

Because my work for the state was temporary I knew eventually I would need to find different employment. When I heard about a new federal prison opening up in a small community about 15 miles away I grudgingly decided to hedge my bets and at least apply there. I was sure I wouldn't end up working there. I mean, would God really call me two thousand miles from my home just to put me back to work at a prison?

When the state decided my time was about up as a probation officer the prison became the most realistic available option. I looked for other work and even thought about going back to the group home, but financially that didn't make sense. So, with about a month left at my state job, I interviewed at the prison. I knew I needed a job, but couldn't believe I was heading back into prison work. I held out hope for some other opportunity, but it didn't happen. I finished my employment with the state on a Friday and on Monday morning drove to what seemed like the middle of nowhere to start at the prison.

While I had been pretty sure the group home work and the probation officer job had not been my calling, it didn't take long before I was absolutely positive that working at the prison wasn't either. The work was not dangerous or even difficult, and I should have just been grateful I had a job. Instead, I was terribly frustrated to be back at a prison.

It's hard to explain the depth of my disliked for this job. Often, while counting sleeping inmates in the middle of the night

I would curse the fact I was doing such monotonous work again. There were many times when I drove home strangling the steering wheel, furious I had left a good day-shift job only to end up working midnight shifts again. I couldn't help thinking if I was going to work in a prison I should have just stayed in California.

A few times I got so angry I even questioned God. I remember thinking, what's going on God? This can't be what you had planned for me.

Because I was unable to understand how returning to prison work could be part of God's plan, my first year working there was the most difficult time up to that point in my spiritual journey. I read once that Satan tempts us to bring out the worst in us, but God tests us to bring out the best in us. I don't know if that's true or not, but I sure felt tested at the time. And it didn't feel like the tests were bringing out the best in me. In fact, at times it felt like I was failing them.

During struggles earlier in recovery with issues like cravings, self-doubt, and even residual physical health concerns, I believed God had provided me with the strength to persevere and that in each difficulty it was only by grace through faith that I had survived. But now, several years into recovery, it was this very faith that seemed to be faltering. I was beginning to doubt the entire idea that God had a plan for me.

I discussed my frustration with Tracy and she encouraged me to be patient and keep praying for guidance. I knew she was right, but I struggled nonetheless. I just couldn't understand why events were going the way they were. It seemed once again I was being pushed about by two competing forces.

Spiritually, even though I didn't understand all the things that were happening, I still felt inclined to stay the course and continue to trust God. But, on a worldly level, I was feeling defeated and ready to just give up. I even thought about moving back to California.

To counter this nagging doubt I increased my daily prayers, asking for more guidance and stronger faith. After a few weeks of intense prayer I was able to take a more objective look at my situation. Seeing things a little more clearly, I realized I had let my pride get in the way of pursuing my purpose. If you've been around recovery a while you've probably heard that ego stands for Edging God Out. Well, that's what I was doing. Rather than listening to God and trusting Him to direct my path, I was trying to force my life to go the way I thought it should.

While I was working through this issue, I received timely help from another one of "those people." He was a supervisor of a different department who came by the visiting room where I was working one evening. He asked how I was doing and I responded by telling him how unhappy I was with my job. He listened for just a short time before interrupting me by saying, "Nobody wants to listen to your complaining. Your best bet would be to keep your mouth shut, do the best work you can, and be happy you have a job."

Of course I didn't appreciate his comments at the time, but after thinking about them for a few days, I realized he had been right—probably more right than he would ever know. What I needed most at the time was a good dose of humility; not only at work, but in all areas of my life. Having been enlightened—however harshly—in subsequent days and weeks I recommitted myself to the hard work of recovery and decided to leave the results of that hard work completely up to God.

I suppose the supervisor's strongly worded advice could be explained as a mere coincidence, but the timing of it was right on. If it had been given a couple of weeks earlier it would have sent me over the edge in anger; a couple of weeks later and it might have been too late. But since I was actively seeking Divine guidance at the time, I was in an ideal position to receive the help which was supplied. I don't know if he was a particularly spiritual man, but I'm convinced God used him to help shake me out of my pride and self-pity.

Once I firmly decided to stay at the prison, I began to explore other positions there and learned that with a bachelor's degree I would qualify for several others including work in case management. This sounded a lot better than continuing to work as a guard. I also figured that with a four year degree I could seek employment elsewhere and eventually leave the prison for more rewarding work.

Already having a two-year degree, I looked for and found a college program which offered an accelerated program in which I could earn a bachelor's degree in 18 months. The problem was the program was going to cost about $15,000, which just happened to be about $15,000 more than we had.

So once again Tracy and I prayed for guidance and ultimately decided it was the right thing to do. I got a student loan, registered for the program, and started classes a couple of months later. Participating in the college courses made me feel like I was doing all I could to prepare for what I believed was God's plan for me.

About a year after I started school a co-worker called me while I was working a housing unit and asked if I was going to put in for the new Drug Counselor position that had just opened up. I immediately answered, "Yes! Yes, I am." I then asked, "What drug counselor position?"

He told me about the position and I almost couldn't believe what I was hearing. I hung up the phone and immediately thought back to my initial interview at the prison and remembered a psychologist on the panel had mentioned some institutions had drug treatment programs. He also said it would be a while before a new facility like ours would have such a program. At the time of the interview, because I figured even if I did get hired I wouldn't be around very long, I hadn't paid much attention to what the doctor said. I was sure paying attention now.

As soon as I could, I called Tracy and told her I was going to be the new drug counselor at the institution. And I was right. Several weeks later the warden called me and told me I'd gotten the job. He knew I didn't have my degree yet, but the fact that I was pursuing it, coupled with my solid work as an officer, was enough for him to choose me. Absent either of these two facts, he probably would have chosen someone else.

Getting this position was for me the culmination of years of working hard and trusting that God was directing my steps. I never thought I would end up back at a prison, but apparently that was part of the plan. I felt so blessed to get the job that I decided right away to do everything in my power to serve Christ well. I had wasted opportunities and potential earlier in my life, but this time I would do my best.

There were no established drug treatment programs when I started in the new position so I essentially got to do whatever I wanted. There was one required drug education course I had to teach, but everything else was up to me. I developed a couple of programs which were a combination of drug education and support group.

In these early groups I let the inmates know I was in recovery, but did not share specific details of my past. I also told them that my recovery was based on my belief in God, but never pushed religion and was always respectful of the men's individual beliefs, whatever they might be. Each day I taught participants the program material that encouraged the development of new life skills and more rational ways of thinking, both standard treatment concepts. But I also told them that for me life only began to change when I finally stopped trying to do things my way and instead turned my life over to God.

Having done only a little work as a group facilitator during an internship in college I probably should have been nervous heading into those first meetings, but I never was. I always made sure I was properly prepared with a lesson plan and also supplemented my preparation with a quick prayer right before the sessions started. Typically it was something as simple as, "God, please help me do this".

Most of the time, even when it didn't seem like I had much to offer that day, I was able to present the group with useful information in a meaningful way. There were plenty of days when I left groups thinking, how the heck did I just do that?

As this continued to happen, I started to believe that right there in those small group rooms, I was being guided by Christ. My budding belief in this was tested on the spot when I was asked to give a presentation in the auditorium to about 125 inmates.

I was down in the front of the auditorium setting up the overhead projector (yes, it was a while ago; no computer, just good old transparencies) as the inmates began to fill the room. I hadn't worked with many of these inmates and knew they wouldn't be the most receptive audience, but I was still feeling confident about doing the presentation. As the last of the men crowded into their seats, an inmate I had known when I was an officer motioned me over to where he sat in the first row. I walked over to see what he needed and he asked, "Hey, Mr. Hall, how do you keep from getting nervous standing down here in front of all these people?"

His words caught me by surprise. I looked up at the mass of men and I thought, that's a darn good question. How am I going to do this? I stood there and suddenly felt very un-confident. I froze for a moment, but regained my composure and spoke from my heart instead of my head. I told the man, "If it was just me standing up here I'd probably freak out. But I trust God is with me so I know I'll do fine."

It was an honest answer, and it helped me to hear those words out loud. I gave the presentation and while it probably wasn't a life-changing event it was pretty good.

My initial programs went well and I felt I was doing what I had been called to do. From the very beginning whenever an inmate made a positive comment about my work I told them what they were seeing was actually God working through me. Years later I heard an inmate who had just received special recognition from a peer say, "It is not me, but my Lord you see." Though I hadn't used these particular words they summed up nicely what I had tried to convey to participants who expressed gratitude in those early programs.

Following one of my first groups an inmate who had been in jail for many years typed out a letter to the warden stating he benefited greatly from the program. At the close of the note he wrote, "God bless Mr. Hall." The warden forwarded the letter to me and it struck me that God had indeed already blessed me. If He hadn't, I might well have ended up the inmate's fellow group member instead of being able to help him as a counselor.

There were plenty of challenges in those early days. One of the toughest was developing therapeutic relationships between inmates who had histories of not trusting prison staff and a prison staff member (me) who had a history of hating inmates. This is one area where I never doubted the presence and power of Divine intervention in my life. Without such help, I would have never developed the compassion needed to work effectively with inmates in the program.

My initial attempt to create these relationships involved developing a good rapport with the men. I figured if we could create a situation where meaningful dialogue could take place we could gain a better understanding of each other. To do this I went in each day and treated the men with respect (and of course required them to treat me, and each other, the same way).

This strategy proved to be easier on some days than others, but was especially difficult when dealing with acting out or defiant inmates. When these situations arose there was a part of me that automatically reverted back to my former more aggressive style of managing inmates.

I repeatedly fought my tendency to just react by trying to handle the situations in a more treatment-oriented manner. I had been given this opportunity by the Lord and believed I was obligated to conduct myself accordingly. Though I definitely made some mistakes along the way and lost my temper more than once, with a large dose of help from the Lord, I was eventually able to create a healthy environment in the groups.

To develop trust and demonstrate that I believed they deserved legitimate treatment, I arrived every day on time with a well prepared lesson plan, ready to get to work. This proved to be effective and in every group at least a few participants mentioned they appreciated the structure and consistency of the program.

Dealing with other staff members' negative attitudes about drug treatment was another considerable challenge. I was proud to be providing treatment and believed good things were happening in the groups, but not everyone was so enthusiastic about the program. Many people thought the program was useless and, honestly, some thought the inmates were too. Some staff members believed the inmates didn't deserve treatment and still others simply did not believe treatment would do the men any good.

These were not all cold-hearted people, many were just skeptical about the value of the program. And the truth was, earlier in my career I had felt the same way. During a budget crisis back in California when staff members were encouraged to submit ideas for saving money, I had suggested the elimination of not only all treatment programs, but all psychological services. (Maybe that I ended up working in a psychology department is pure irony, but I believe it just shows how much God can change our lives.)

Such skepticism was not at all unwarranted. There were plenty of legitimate reasons to be leery of programs like mine. Because participants have different motives for being there, any drug treatment can be tricky. But drug treatment in prison, where inmates often get a sentence reduction for completing a program, can be especially difficult.

Many who participate in prison programs have no real interest in treatment or sobriety. They simply want to get out of jail earlier. They mock the system by faking their way through treatment and then go home virtually unchanged. Everyone is aware of this to some degree and it makes it very difficult to develop and maintain legitimate prison-based programs.

Encountering disapproving comments from other staff reminded me once again that my environment, that is, the people and the events in the world around me, was not always going to be supportive of what I believed was supposed to be accomplished in my life. To counter this negativity, I remained focused on the real reason I was there and tried to limit interaction with anyone who did not appreciate our program. This worked well, but negative comments from others, both staff and inmates, would be a significant concern later in my career.

I truly believe some men benefited from those initial groups and others at least became more open-minded toward recovery. I never operated under the illusion that everyone was being helped or even that most of them really wanted to change.

But rather than focus on the uninterested men, I chose to put energy into those who were seeking help. I guess you could say I followed the old adage that's provided encouragement to helping professionals for years, "If I can help even one person…"

I never thought God put me there to change the entire world. I believed I was there to help men the same way I had been helped ten years earlier. Every time I witnessed a man change, not be cured, but changed to some degree, I became more convinced God's work was being accomplished in those austere prison group rooms.

After running various support groups and education

classes for about 18 months, I learned our institution was going to get a long-term drug treatment program. This would involve more intense and more comprehensive treatment. Previously, treatment groups had consisted of only hour-long meetings, which met once-a-week and lasted for a couple months. Now, inmates would have the opportunity to participate in a daily treatment program that lasted nine months.

I was happy to learn about the new program and it seemed to be a shot in the arm (maybe not the best expression to use when talking about drug treatment) which served to re-energize me. I prepared myself by reading more treatment related literature and studying the program materials I had received in advance of the program starting.

In addition to this worldly preparation, I also prayed to God for the strength and wisdom to serve Him well in this new assignment; a new assignment for which I had been waiting many years.

There were a few mandatory components of the new program (i.e., using assigned workbooks, completing a certain number of hours, and meeting in a designated area) but the day-to-day functioning and how the treatment would be presented was left up to me. My supervisor (a wonderful psychologist who supported me completely) was content to set me up with a meeting area and turn me loose. It was an awesome opportunity. I had a long-term drug program which I could run almost any way I wanted. I felt blessed to be in such a situation and often thanked God for the opportunity.

The first program I facilitated was a wonderful experience and probably the most meaningful of the 10 long-term groups (called cohorts) I would eventually complete while working with the men. This initial group wasn't without its rough spots though, especially in the early going. Because we were doing everything for the first time each day had the potential to be a very good day or a not so good day.

A few days into the first program an inmate who was apparently agitated by my lack of familiarity with program materials sarcastically asked me in front of the group how long I had been facilitating the program. I told him, "About three days."

He quickly replied, "So you really don't know what you're doing do you?"

I shot back, "No, I don't. But you don't have to worry about it, because if you don't like it you can pick up your stuff and get the heck out of here." (I may have used more colorful language than that. Sometimes, even with God's help, old habits die hard.) Though it caused a considerable disruption to the group, this exchange served a useful purpose. It was vitally important for the men to know I was sincerely interested in helping them, but they also needed to know I would be in full charge of the group. Incidents like this gave me the opportunity to make clear how things were going to work.

Many of the men appreciated my approach. Inmates often feel like they have little control over their environment and are troubled by the chaos that goes on around them. Over the years it was clear that participants who were uncomfortable (or even scared) in other areas of the prison were more at ease in our group rooms. I always thought this was one small way God worked through me to help men who had been relegated to an insignificant existence inside the prison.

One of the most important and effective aspects of that first group was the degree to which we explored and discussed spiritual issues. We talked openly about faith and its role in recovery. Nobody had religion pushed on them and men with other beliefs, or no particular beliefs at all, were always heard and respected. As the program progressed, many participants stated the spiritual component of our daily work was the area from which they were benefiting the most.

I prayed and sought God's guidance often during that first cohort. I shared with the men my faith and the fact I was in recovery. I did my best each day to provide them with an example of someone who, with Christ's help, had overcome addiction. I told them, "If I can do it, you can do it. I'm no better or worse than you. And I am no more deserving of God's blessings than you are."

I never preached to them or boasted about being sober. What I did was tell them what I believed to be true, what I would tell all subsequent groups; if they would trust God and work hard they could achieve and maintain meaningful sobriety in their lives.

I doubt anyone was completely cured during that first cohort, but meaningful changes occurred in some of the men's lives. Several participants stated it had been a life-altering experience. Others reported less dramatic but still positive results. Some stated they had learned to look at life differently, some said they had regained self-respect by being treated like a man, and some simply stated they would at least consider sobriety as an option in their future, something they had never done before.

Maybe the best thing about that first group was when a young participant approached me on the last day and said, "Thanks Mr. Hall for helping me become a man."

I thanked him for the kind words, but suggested he had done all the work. I also told him any help that came from me was just God working through me.

In drug treatment there are no big bonuses or promotions for good work. There are no awards or trophies for helping people change. Receiving comments like those from that young man is about as good as the rewards get. But, hearing how he felt was good enough for me. In fact, his words were as good as anything I could think of. Christ had reached out to him and just happened to use me in the process. And being a part of that was awesome.

The second cohort was another positive experience. The men were similar to those in the first group in that they came from various backgrounds and had differing levels of interest in treatment. I tried to provide the same structure, guidance and hope which seemed to help the first group. Although not all of the men sincerely committed to a life of sobriety, just like in the first group, several men were truly changed by their work in the program.

At the end of the group one of the men presented me with a drawing which he said summarized my work with the group. He initially had been quite critical of my work and cynical about the value of the program. But, as he wrote in a brief note which accompanied the drawing, he eventually came to believe I sincerely cared about and wanted to help the men in the group. He said by sharing my experiences I had provided them with a living example that change was possible.

It had taken me ten years, but I was finally able to give to a few men what I had needed most when I was hurting; hope. Hope that life could be different. Hope that they didn't have to die addicted or in jail. And practically every day I had tried to ensure they knew from where that hope came. If the drawing was any indication, they had clearly understood. It was a penciled portrait of me above the words, "Trust God and Work Hard". The drawing hung on my office wall for years (accompanied only by a swaying-hips Elvis clock).

By the end of the second group, I had reached a point in my life where I was serving as a channel for the Lord as He worked through me to help men who many people deemed unworthy of help or as simply incapable of being helped. I saw it differently and actually felt privileged to be involved in a process which brought about significant, meaningful change in men's lives. I felt truly blessed to be working where I was, doing what I was, and helping those I was able to help.

I was amazed at how far God had taken me. I had been saved from my self-destructive addicted lifestyle, was returned to health, met and married the best woman a man could ever hope for, became a father to two beautiful kids, and was given the privilege of starting a drug treatment program. People had seemingly come out of nowhere to help me along the way and one situation after another (even if I didn't see it at the time) had moved me closer and closer to my goal of serving God by helping others. Though I still experienced challenges in my life, I firmly believed I was following the path which had been laid out for me.

It seemed to me that, in an expression I heard back then, I had been blessed beyond measure.

PART 2
Saved From Myself

CHAPTER 5

A Prideful Fall

With God's help, in the ten years following treatment I had won several spiritual battles in the ongoing conflict between my call to live according to His plan and the pull of things of this world. I won my battle with addiction, overcame hatred with compassion, and beat back nagging doubt with a faith that allowed me to continue to pursue His will.

I would love for this story to proceed uninterrupted to a happy ending in which I ultimately triumph in this inner conflict and spend the rest of my life serving the Lord, but it does not.

Even as I was being guided forward, and felt strong in many areas of my life, there continued within a war between the spiritual and the natural. Despite the incredible gifts I received from God, I was unable to achieve a lasting victory over worldly desires. Though He provided everything I needed to continue my walk with Him and remain upright in my recovery, I gave into the world and stumbled again.

Of the numerous factors which contributed to this fall, I have identified two primary areas where I succumbed to the pull of earthly concerns. Hardly unique to my situation, these are two of the three areas identified two thousand years ago by the apostle John when he warned us about loving the things of this world. He listed pleasures of the flesh, lust of the eyes, and boastful pride.

My problems began when rather than continuing to surrender my life to Christ, I became prideful and resumed the pursuit of man-made pleasures. I have given these two issues considerable thought and developed a reasonable understanding of how they led to my falling again.

Few human traits play a more integral role in the development and progression of addiction than boastful pride. It blinds people to clear signs substance use is beginning to cause them problems and encourages them to discount the concerns of caring family and friends who recognize the same troubling issues. As addiction progresses the prideful addict insists that despite how bad the situation is getting, they are in complete control. An extreme close-mindedness develops which seals the addict off from the truth and lets them create their own understanding of reality.

In the late stages of addiction, pride may be the last thing an addict holds on to. It causes them to reject responsibility for the painfully obvious damage caused by their substance use and to instead blame others for the problems. This distorted thinking is best exemplified by the classic retort of many alcoholics who, when confronted about their drinking reply, "The only problem with my drinking is all you people who won't stop bothering me about it."

This line (or some variation of it) is so common that every time I have shared it with a treatment group at least several participants have nodded their heads and smiled. They have heard or said the same thing before.

At this point those familiar with addiction might ask, if boastful pride is so common in later-stage addiction, what about the addicts who report feeling worthless as they slide further into their addiction? How can these people be both prideful and feel terrible about themselves at the same time? Rationally this would not seem to make sense, but addiction is anything but rational. This paradox of feeling two different ways at once is actually quite common and in recovery circles is described by the phrase, "Addicts are egomaniacs with inferiority complexes."

For many addicts feelings of superiority coexist with a strong sense of inferiority. And so they unfortunately move deeper into addiction as a result of both boastful pride and feelings of worthlessness.

Unhealthy pride also plays a large role in two of the best known traits of addiction; denial and hitting bottom. As discussed earlier, I have never believed that denial renders an addict unable to see the damage caused by their drug use. It is much more a case of being unwilling to see what is happening and pride is the driving force behind this unwillingness. Until the pride is broken, the person remains unwilling to acknowledge reality. Hitting bottom is essentially when the addict's life gets so messed up that not even their false pride (denial) can keep them from acknowledging how bad things are.

It is only when pride is overcome that most addicts are willing to admit that their lives have bottomed out.

Just as pride can drive a person deeper into addiction, it can also serve as a major roadblock to recovering from addiction. If an addict remains boastfully proud during an attempt at sobriety--even if it includes the best available treatment--they are unlikely to succeed. Recovery is all about practicing humility and learning new ways of living. And as the saying goes, it is impossible to teach anything to the person who thinks they know everything.

Pride was clearly recognized as a problem by the founders of AA and it has even been suggested that the first three steps; admitting we are powerless, believing a power greater than us can help, and turning our lives over to that power, all directly address the need to eliminate boastful pride. Whether this assessment is completely accurate or not, I have always thought this a good indication of the significant obstacle pride can present to sobriety.

During my descent into addiction and the early stages of treatment, pride had caused me all the problems listed above and more. But by the time I left the facility my worldly pride had blessedly been replaced with a spiritual humility which proved to be essential for my recovery. This humility was severely tested during my work as a guard at the new prison when, as described earlier, my prideful attitude rose up in direct opposition to my desire to follow Christ's call.

Fortunately, with God's help my spiritual calling prevailed in the battle against pride and I continued along the path He had lit for me, eventually ending up in the very position for which I had prayed.

Unfortunately, beginning about two years into my new work in the treatment program, pride again reared its ugly head and the conflict resumed. While pride didn't suddenly render me unable to maintain recovery or incapable of providing meaningful treatment, what it did do was make me overconfident and careless in important areas of my life. And this time it would produce nearly catastrophic results.

The first area impacted was my study of addiction. For ten years I had committed myself to learning all I could in order to remain sober. I had also begun to utilize this collected knowledge in my early treatment programs and eventually became justly confident in my understanding of addiction. Troublingly, as I became more prideful I started to think I knew all there was to know about keeping myself sober and began to view any subsequent learning as something I would be doing for the benefit of the men in treatment.

I was becoming a man who thought he knew everything and, of course, as this happened I stopped learning the valuable lessons I needed to stay sober.

Maybe even worse than over-confidence in my knowledge of addiction was the arrogance I began to show toward ongoing recovery. In my groups I had always defined humility as understanding that "the rules of life apply to me." It was a concept we repeatedly explored and I often shared personal examples of how humility had served me well early in my recovery. It is particularly troubling to look back and recognize I took one of the most fundamental concepts I was teaching the men and totally disregarded it in my own life.

As my pride increased, I put humility on the shelf and started to view some of the rules of life (specifically rules of recovery) as not applying to me. For instance, though I knew how dangerous it was for recovering addicts to spend too much time thinking about getting high, I began to daydream about drinking again. At a time when I should have been focusing solely on ways to grow in my recovery, my mind would wander to thoughts about how good a drink or two might be.

Vivid memories of the dark days of my addiction kept me from glamorizing past drinking experiences (a common problem for many addicts who begin to lose focus on sobriety). I remembered exactly how bad it was.

What I did instead of romanticizing past drinking, was to think if I did drink again it would be different than those awful times in the past. And anyone familiar with addiction will tell you there are few thoughts more dangerous for a person in recovery than "this time it will be different."

When these thoughts first came, I was able to shake them off as silly old addicted thinking. I knew better than to think like that. This created a peculiar problem in that each time I successfully discredited such thoughts, my overconfidence increased in a strange, paradoxical way. I would tell myself that my ability to identify unhealthy thinking was a clear indication I was sharp enough to not have to worry about such thinking. (Hello, distorted thinking.)

Shortly after the end of my second 9-month group, these thoughts became more frequent and I was less able to shrug them off as the nonsense they were. Eventually, it got to where I erroneously believed someone like me--you know, a guy who knew just about everything there was to know about recovery--could safely drink again. One of my main selling points (in addition to believing it would be different this time) was to convince myself if I was to drink again my immense knowledge of addiction would surely enable me to detect if anything started to go wrong.

The most troubling aspect of this situation was it happened during a time when I was spending each working day teaching other addicts to avoid the very thoughts I was thinking. I actually presented some of the thinking mistakes I was making as examples of what the participants needed to avoid. I was professionally encouraging one way of thinking while doing the exact opposite in my private life.

Writing this now, I still scratch my head and wonder what I was thinking. The only explanation I have come up with is the incredible power of worldly pride.

The second area in which I succumbed to the pull of earthly concerns was seeking worldly pleasure instead of being satisfied with the happiness I had found in the many blessings of sobriety. Early in recovery, I experienced joy in even the most basic everyday experiences.

I remember once just after treatment, driving down my sister's street, a road traveled hundreds of times, and noticing how beautiful the palm trees were in the fading sunlight. As I walked up to her house, I realized it wasn't only the beauty of the trees, but also the fact that I was sober enough to appreciate them. It had been years since I'd been in her neighborhood at this time of the evening sober. It was such a simple thing and yet it felt so good. During those early years there were many times I experienced joy merely from the fact that whatever I was doing, I was doing it sober.

In addition to enjoying such simple pleasures, I had experienced great satisfaction in many areas of my life. Meeting my wife and starting our family were the most rewarding experiences of my life and I felt blessed when given the opportunity to help others through treatment.

These blessings and others left me very content with the level of happiness and pleasure in my life until an event about five years into recovery. This incident triggered a part of me that had remained dormant since treatment and sparked in me a desire for man-made, worldly pleasure. Though I did not see it as a big deal at the time, I firmly believe it was a primary factor in my fall.

It happened just before we left California when I damaged my shoulder diving for a ball during a softball tournament in Palm Springs. It was a painful injury so I went to a doctor and he prescribed some powerful pain medication (Vicodin) which I had never used before. I took the initial dose as directed, but when my shoulder was still hurting a couple of hours later I decided to take two more pills. This proved to be a big mistake.

Those second two pills hit me like a ton of bricks. First, I got light headed and then everything started to slow down. I realized I had taken too much medication and, feeling like I was about to pass out, decided to call my nephew. He got to my house and when he asked how I was feeling I said something to the effect of, "I think I'm high."

We were both unfamiliar with the effects of Vicodin (as neither of us had messed around much with prescription drugs) and weren't sure what to do. So we did what many men do when they are in a jam and don't know what to do; we called a woman.

Tracy came straight home from work and found me on the couch almost asleep. She called the hospital, explained my situation and was told the amount taken was not dangerous and that I would be fine just sleeping it off. She was instructed to check on me every so often, which she did, and there were no further problems. But something significant happened that afternoon.

After having been completely sober for five years I had suddenly experienced the feeling of being high again. My brain remembered that feeling and liked it. I failed to recognize the importance of this experience and when I used the rest of the Vicodin and subsequent prescriptions for similar medications (for other sports injuries and chronic back pain) I didn't view it as a problem. I simply told myself I was using the medication for legitimate pain (even though the level of pain often did not require such medicine) and figured as long as it made my back, shoulder, or neck hurt less, the fact it also made me a little euphoric was just an added bonus.

Looking back, I now realize there was a problem with my use of pain medication. Unrecognized at the time however was the fact that I was slowly developing a preference, which grew with each subsequent use of the medication, in which my brain began to favor the artificial euphoria provided by chemicals to the natural highs enjoyed earlier in recovery. This budding preference initially seemed non-problematic, but it clearly became a serious problem a couple years later when, like so many other recovering people, I started to get bored with recovery.

My displeasure with recovery started subtly, as I became generally less satisfied with the sober lifestyle (a condition sometimes described as being secretly disappointed with sobriety). Over time, I grew impatient waiting for the occasional positive rewards of helping others and found less enjoyment in the simple daily pleasures of recovery.

Even as I continued to experience countless blessings in my life, I began to question if I was ever going to get to feel as good as I had while drinking. My pride contributed to the problem by leading me to think with all the hard work I was doing, I deserved to feel "good".

Inexplicably, having a drink was beginning to make pretty good sense to me.

As powerful as the pull of the world was, I'm convinced I could have avoided falling had I remained steadfast in my walk with the Lord. Anchored in faith, I would have continued to challenge boastful pride with healthy humility. Instead of pursuing worldly pleasure, solid in faith, I would have remained content with the many blessings in my life. Unfortunately, I broke free of my strong ties to the Lord and slowly began to drift.

It has been said that the closer you walk with Christ, the less room there is for anything to come in between. By getting off track in my faith, I created an opening for things of this world, especially worldly pride, to come in between God and me.

One important example of this was in my prayer life. I had kept praying daily for my family, friends, and the men in treatment, but prayers regarding my sobriety began to change. Earlier I had prayed several times a day specifically about recovery and considered prayer the cornerstone of my sobriety. I started each day with, "God please help me stay clean and sober", and finished the day by thanking Him for helping me through it.

Now however, I was praying less intensely and less intentionally for guidance and strength in sobriety. I was setting myself up for a fall by depending less on prayer and more on my prideful understanding to guide me through life.

There were other signs I was slowly distancing myself from Christ. I left treatment with the goal of being like a sponge, soaking up all available spiritual wisdom He provided. I had listened for His voice and found it in literature and sermons, through people I knew, and even strangers on the street. Now, to my own detriment, I began to listen more to worldly voices and less to His. I read fewer spiritually centered books and instead read books about sports, politics, history, and finance. I reached out less to other people of faith and withdrew back into the more private existence of my earlier life.

What I am describing here was not a complete turning away from Christ. It was not like that. I continued to believe in God and tried to live accordingly. I never abandoned God and, of course, He never abandoned me. What I did was allow worldly concerns to create a breach between us.

Over the course of a few years, even as I appeared to be doing quite well, I had slowly created my own perfect storm. I had come to believe I knew all there was to know about addiction and that if I were to drink again it would be different than in the past. I had begun to prefer artificial pleasure to the authentic joy sobriety had brought into my life. I had convinced myself I deserved to feel as good as I had when drinking.

Most importantly, I had drifted in my walk with the Lord. I separated from the very foundation of my recovery and started to rely on myself. Though I was still interested in riding the tandem bike with Christ, I decided I was ready to do the driving.

On a Saturday afternoon a week before Christmas 2000 I did drive. Of my own accord, and with absolutely no rational reason to do so, I left a basketball game and drove to a liquor store where I bought a bottle of alcohol. I had succumbed to the things of this world and convinced myself it would be ok to have a drink, and that's exactly what I did.

CHAPTER 6

Drifting Back Into Despair

Have you ever had one of those friends you can go a long time without seeing and when you finally get together again, your relationship picks up right where it left off, almost like you were never apart? If you have, then you have a good idea of what happened when I had that first drink. There was nothing novel or intriguing about it. It was the same comforting feeling I had a thousand times before. I was amazed at how little had changed.

It was as if the ten-plus years since my last drink had never existed.

Though I possess a powerful memory and an almost uncanny ability to remember dates, I cannot recall the next time I drank. I'm convinced this is because after that first drink, the next time didn't really matter. From that day forward, I was a drinker again. I didn't start drinking, nor would I ever resume drinking, nearly as much or as often as before, but as soon as we were reacquainted, I welcomed my old friend back into my life for what would be a five year stay.

The factors involved in my decision to start drinking again have already been described, and while both boastful pride and the pursuit of worldly pleasure would have an ongoing role in my decision to continue drinking, they were strongly supported by an ill-conceived strategy that led me right back into self-destructive behavior.

My plan was to divide my life into various sections. Before ever taking a drink I had started to do this in my prayer life by leaving mention of my recovery out of my talks with God. Now, I was going a step further by trying to take certain parts of my physical life and separate them from my spiritual life. I would put drinking and the behaviors needed to support it (i.e., dishonesty, manipulation, deception) into isolated compartments which I would not share with God. These issues I would manage on my own.

I never fully recognized how weak and foolish this strategy was until years later when I read Billy Graham's book *The Journey* and for the first time fully understood that to follow Christ we have to surrender our entire life to Him.

The concept of complete surrender makes complete sense when you consider the alternative. I mean, can we really hope to commit certain areas of our life to God while trying to keep other parts hidden? Despite how obviously flawed this concept now appears, when I began to drink again, I really believed I could keep parts of my life hidden from God.

I am not suggesting I invented this strategy or that I'm the only one to ever think this way. If you are a person of faith who has struggled with addiction (or some other issue you tried to keep to yourself) this might sound painfully familiar. If that is the case then you already know what a terribly ineffective plan it is. If you are not familiar with it, let me say not only is it a poor strategy for spiritual living, it is also a recipe for trouble.

In addition to trying to keep my drinking separate from my

relationship with God, I also attempted to keep it hidden from other people. As would be the case if I was hiding any behavior, this required me to be less than completely honest with others.

The one and maybe only time I was entirely straightforward was a couple days after that first drink when I told Tracy the truth about what I had done. She was concerned, but based on what she knew there was really no reason to be alarmed. She never knew me back when I was drinking and over the previous decade had come to know me as a rational and responsible person. The conversation with Tracy was the last time I was completely honest with her, or anyone else (including myself), about my drinking.

I did not have to develop new ways of hiding my drinking; all I had to do was revive old techniques mastered earlier in my life.

The most basic strategy used was drinking alone. I almost never drank around other people and always took steps to ensure that no one knew I had been drinking. This was done by being careful about when, where, and what I drank (all alcohol smells but some is much less pungent than others). I also made strategic use of standard tools of the trade, including eye drops, mouthwash, breath mints, and chewing gum. One classic but almost entirely ineffective technique I avoided was the use of strong cologne to cover the smell of alcohol. I always thought it was a careless way to draw the attention of others and that was the last thing I wanted to do.

On the rare occasions when I did drink around others I only had a drink or two. This is an age-old ploy of secretive heavy drinkers. Most people pay little attention to somebody having a couple of beers, a mixed drink, or glass of wine. What draws attention is excessive drinking and drunkenness. That's what people notice.

So the key is to avoid acting drunk (another skill I had perfected in my earlier drinking days) and limit the drinking done in front of others. That doesn't mean you actually drink less, it just means you find ways of drinking more without others knowing.

There are a number of ways to do this, but one of the more commonly used techniques around the home is sometimes referred to as garage or closet drinking. (The same basic technique is used in many other social and even professional settings.) It goes something like this; in order to keep the extent of their drinking undercover an individual stashes alcohol some place in the house, often in the garage, basement, or back room. While participating in ordinary activities around the house (which may or may not include drinking) they repeatedly sneak away to get a drink.

The effectiveness of this kind of drinking varies widely. Often everybody in the house knows what is going on but doesn't say anything for fear of starting an argument. Other times people are aware of the drinking but remain quiet out of apathy or resignation. In other cases this technique is extremely effective and may go virtually undetected for years.

I'm ashamed to say I used this technique and as embarrassing as it is to admit, judging by the genuine surprise of family and friends when I finally told them I had started drinking again, I was good at it.

In acknowledging my ability to conceal the drinking, I must admit it did not require Houdini-like skills. It wasn't like people were following me around or watching my every move just waiting for me to slip up and drink. I had been sober for over ten years and moved halfway across the country. The vast majority of people I knew never gave a second thought as to whether or not I drank. To those who did become aware of my (what they believed to be) very limited drinking it was a non-issue. These people never knew me as a drunk and had no reason to be concerned. But I was concerned, and though I was able to keep the extent of my drinking hidden from others, I couldn't hide it from myself. And I knew it wasn't right.

Drinking required me to be dishonest and from the very

first drink I don't ever remember feeling good about it. I'm not talking about feeling good as a result of consuming alcohol (that happened all the time), I mean feeling good about drinking. In the early years of my recovery and spiritual growth I learned to listen to my conscience like never before. My attunement to this inner voice (which I believe to be the Holy Spirit) helped me stay on track through many difficult and tempting situations. When I started drinking again, the dishonesty required to facilitate it did not sit well with my conscience.

I also knew on a deeper level that drinking was wrong because it distracted me from the path God had planned for my life. I believed in addition to raising my family, I had been saved in order to help others. I knew drinking was not part of this plan and virtually every time I drank I felt the strong tugging of my conscience urging me to stop.

Unfortunately I disregarded these inner warnings, either by just putting them out of my mind or by pridefully telling myself it would not be like before because I now knew what I was doing and could handle it. It was this refusal to accept God's guidance through the Holy Spirit within me that led to trouble. By choosing to go it alone, I was unable to fight off the powerful pull of worldly desires and continued to drink.

During the first few years of drinking I experienced almost no external problems. In fact, during this time I was living a blessed life. My relationship with my family was good, we were all healthy, and we enjoyed our time together. We had a comfortable home, were stable financially, and I was in good standing and well-respected in my career. But eventually, this seemingly trouble-free drinking would end.

The first place I detected external negative consequences of drinking was at my job. Though no one else ever said anything about it, I noticed a decline in my performance and in the general quality of my treatment program.

It is difficult to determine exactly what part my drinking played in the decreased effectiveness of the program because it coincided with several other factors beyond my control. However, it is reasonable to say drinking compromised my ability to provide quality treatment and this certainly impacted the program.

The time was the fall of 2001, and immediately following the attacks of September 11, all treatment staff members were directed to be extra sensitive to issues related to religion or spirituality. We had participants of various faiths and as such were instructed to avoid promotion of any particular belief system. Soon there began an effort to remove spirituality from our program material. The inmates were still afforded ample opportunity to participate in religious activities through chapel programs at the institution, but over the next few years, each time our drug treatment literature was updated, spirituality was given less and less attention until it was completely removed from program material.

In truth, it wasn't just the removal of spiritual concerns from our material. As I drifted from Christ my presentation of the program became less spiritually-centered. Of course I had never preached to the men, but in the first couple of cohorts I had definitely brought a spiritual presence to the group. This aspect of the program decreased as I drifted and I was probably as responsible as anyone for the reduced role of spirituality in the program.

Accompanying these changes was a significant decrease in the level of commitment of the participants. Initially our program was small and fortunately the first two groups included a good number of men who were sincerely interested in sobriety and based their recovery on an active spirituality. There was also a newness to the program that helped create a high energy level in the groups. All of these elements combined to make a healthy treatment environment.

However, as the program expanded to several cohorts at a time, and the novelty of it diminished, we lost much of the positive energy. The spiritual component dissipated and our program began to slip into a perfunctory process where an increasing number of participants were less interested in meaningful treatment and much more interested in merely completing the program in order to get out of prison early. These changes did not occur overnight and it wasn't like the program suddenly became totally ineffective.   There continued to be success stories, and in most cohorts at least a couple of men stated that the program helped them change their lives, but it was clearly different.

I had always been realistic about the limited number of men being helped and figured if several guys in each group benefited it was worth the effort. But as the spiritual aspect faded out, and the men became less sincere, there were cohorts where I felt like I spent the better part of a year working for only one or maybe two guys.

I continued to provide adequate treatment but was not in a strong position to meet the challenges of our changing program. Early in my work I had benefited greatly by following the "Trust God and work hard" philosophy. I had relied directly on His strength to help me through daily challenges. Now, though I was still working hard, I was no longer fully trusting God.

When I separated my sobriety from my spiritual life I also began to rely less on spiritual guidance in my work. I was uncomfortable praying for help in providing treatment to others when I was not willing to ask for help in my own sobriety, so for a time I quit seeking guidance in both. As a result I was less able to maintain a high level of enthusiasm for, and commitment to, providing treatment. And as the conditions in the program continued to deteriorate I was more susceptible to distractions and discouragement.

This was most evident to me during two particular instances that earlier in my career would have been met with resolve and determination, but now brought out in me disillusionment and doubt.

The first incident occurred when a former participant came into my office while I was preparing for the next day's group. Seeing books and papers spread across my desk he asked what I was doing. When I told him, he laughed and said that many inmates wondered why I worked so hard when the program was such a joke. As inciting as these words were, the situation was made even worse by the fact this guy was serving time for child-porn, which put him squarely at the bottom of the inmate pecking order. So, in addition to dealing with criticism of the program, I had to hear it from someone whom even other inmates found reprehensible. It's probably enough to simply say, my response to him was not very Christian-like.

Afterward, I was angry about what he had said, but also frustrated because I knew there was some truth in it. I had always known the program was not held in high regard by others but had been able to ignore their opinions by remaining focused on what I knew Christ had led me there to do. But now, seething in my office, I was unable to shake off his negative comments and it made me doubt the work I was doing.

The second incident happened several months later on a frigid day when the institution was expecting a new inmate of great interest. He had been involved in one of the huge financial scandals of the 2000s, and his arrival was a big enough deal that several national news organizations sent crews to the prison the day of his scheduled arrival. I remember seeing reporters parked on farmland across the street from the main entrance when I drove in and then again when I left that evening. For some reason the inmate did not show up and the reporters spent a day in the cold for nothing.

A couple days later I came across a blog by one of the reporters, apparently written at the end of that first day. Judging by his comments he had not enjoyed his sampling of the local climate. His message, dripping with contempt, began with something like, "Standing here in a farmer's frozen field somewhere in the middle of nowhere . . . ."

I know this sounds trivial or even petty, but his spiteful

description of the institution, a place to which I had committed myself and worked hard at for several years, really hit me hard. When I was a kid I had dreams of one day playing in Dodger Stadium, Wrigley Field, or Fenway Park. Instead, I ended up working in a farmer's frozen field?

If I had been in a better place spiritually and been practicing healthy humility, I would not have given this another thought. However, coming at a time when I was prideful in my thoughts, less stable in my faith, and beginning to doubt what I was doing in my work, this felt like a punch in the stomach.

During the time I drank, my program became less and less effective. Certainly I was not to blame for the entire situation, but by failing to completely accept the blessing and guidance of God, I had become less able to perform the work I had been called to do. Though I continued to exceed worldly standards (i.e., receiving outstanding work evaluations), I faltered in my spiritual commitment to help others and the program suffered as a result.

After about three years of drinking, a big part of me knew what I was doing was wrong. I knew it was getting in the way of pursuing my God-given purpose. I even knew that it was likely to get worse. Yet because I was operating from a position of arrogant pride, another part of me continued to rationalize drinking by believing that because I hadn't experienced any significant external trouble I didn't have a problem.

As I moved into the last two years of drinking, my ability to rationalize and justify drinking would be severely tested. This was particularly true when I began to experience debilitating hangovers. I had been able to minimize the problems at work by suggesting they were caused by various factors, but the hangovers, conditions caused directly and exclusively by drinking, made it much more difficult to deny there was a problem.

The easiest way to determine if you have a problem with alcohol or other drugs is to ask a single question; does the substance use ever cause problems? Over the years I have administered hundreds of lengthy substance abuse assessments and found these interviews to be helpful. But if a person can be completely honest they shouldn't need an hour long assessment to determine if there is a problem. The simple question, "Does substance use cause problems?" is all they need. If they can honestly answer no, they are probably ok. If they answer yes, well then, they have a problem.

Pretty simple. If use causes problems, it's a problem.

By this reliable standard, the hangovers alone were proof I had developed a problem with drinking. They often left me drained of the energy I needed to be productive and too many days that could have been spent pursuing my purpose were spent dealing with the negative after-effects of drinking. As my drinking progressed, it became evident the hangovers and work issues were not the only problems. Drinking was also leading to poor decisions and careless actions in other areas of my life, and these choices and behaviors were gradually pulling me away from being the person I knew God wanted me to be.

It was during this period I started telling myself each time I drank that it would be the last time, a clear indication I knew there was a problem. If I had truly viewed my drinking as non-problematic, I would have had no need to swear off drinking each time I did it.

All these factors combined to provide me with irrefutable evidence I had a problem. However, instead of admitting it and stopping as I had said I would if a problem was ever recognized, I clung to the belief I was still in control. I now vainly vowed I would stop drinking if it ever caused any "big" problems or if things got "really bad." (If the image of a man digging a deeper and deeper hole comes to mind, you have it about right).

This bizarre paradox of telling myself that I had everything under control while simultaneously telling myself that each drink needed to be the last speaks to how distorted my thinking was again becoming. And this silly bit of mental gymnastics did nothing except allow me to drink longer and dig a deeper hole for myself.

❖ ❖ ❖

Looking back at this part of my life I have often asked myself why. Why did I keep drinking?

After much thought, I now believe it was more than just boastful pride, the pursuit of worldly pleasure, and distorted thinking. Somewhere along the way I started to feel that old empty feeling again. As I drifted in my faith and lost my close connection to Christ, the God-shape hole in my soul, the wound that had plagued me earlier in life, was re-opened. As the feelings of emptiness increased, I once again tried to sooth the wound with chemicals, falsely believing they would make me feel better.

A second question I have sometimes asked is why I didn't ask others for help? With the benefit of hindsight, I know the simple answer is pride. Even as circumstances got worse, I continued to tell myself I could handle it. My pride eliminated the option of seeking professional help; that simply was not going to happen. It also kept me from asking people who cared about me for help. The situation with those close to me was complicated by the very practical concern of just who I would have asked. Because I had been so efficient at hiding my drinking, nobody had any idea that I was struggling. As such, I was hesitant to blindside any of them with the news I had a problem with alcohol again

One question I have never had to ask was why I did not turn to Christ?

Though I knew at the time I should go to God in prayer and ask for help with my drinking, I did not believe I could. By then I had begun to feel so ashamed of my behavior (i.e., drinking, dishonesty, and drifting from Him) I did not feel right asking Him for help, especially with something from which I had once already been saved.

I thought of my situation this way: Imagine a happily married couple in which one partner destroys the loving relationship by being unfaithful. When this comes to light, even though that partner broke their vow and dishonored their spouse, the spouse completely forgives and takes them back. Not secretly harboring ill-will or resentment; but rather fully loving and trusting their partner again. The relationship is completely restored and made even better than before. Then the same partner cheats again. This is how I felt I had acted toward Christ and it is why I did not turn to Him for help.

During 2005, the last year of drinking, my enthusiasm for work continued to decline and reached its all-time low one day after the final session of a difficult and non-productive group. Following the last meeting I walked into my supervisor's office and said something like, "Well, that's a year of my life I wish I had back."

The situation got so bad I had even begun to pray again for help in getting the program back up to par for the men. Not unlike all those years earlier, I could pray for others but I was unwilling or unable to pray for myself.

The last few months of that year were marked by two events that finally shattered any prideful illusion I had about having everything under control. The first occurred on a Monday during the fall. I had celebrated my birthday over the weekend and drank more than usual. When I got to work I felt fine, but as the day went on my hands began to shake noticeably; at least enough that I noticed.

Now, I could have come up with any number of explanations for this (i.e., blood sugar off due to tons of sweets the day before, hungry because I hadn't eaten all day, or just fatigued from lack of sleep) and most would have been partially true. But by now I was no longer interested in these ridiculous head games. I knew the reason my hands were shaking was because of the alcohol. Though no one around me would have likely noticed my condition, I cancelled my afternoon group and went home.

This event was a turning point in that I could no longer kid myself into believing I would quit if things got "really bad". By virtually any measure I could think of, being physically unable to do my job was really bad. And, when I drank again a short time later, I knew I wasn't going to quit.

For the first time, I admitted the facts of the case indicated (much like earlier in my life) I would be into this drinking thing for the long haul. A small part of me insisted I would still be ok, that I was still in control. But even that small part would be crushed before the year was over.

The second event was easily the low point of this period of my life (and maybe my entire life). It was the day after Christmas and we decided to take a group of family and friends shopping. I drank earlier in the day but gave no thought to it when I volunteered to drive. While my blood alcohol content was likely well below the legal limit, there was no denying I was impaired when I decided to drive.

With my daughter and her best friend in the car, we laughed and sang with the radio as we headed down the highway. I actually remember thinking at the time how much I loved those kids. When we got to our exit I approached a roundabout (a road design that allows cars coming off the freeway to merge, while yielding, into traffic instead of stopping) and proceeded directly into the circle.

Failing to yield, I pulled directly into the path of a speeding vehicle. I never saw it coming.

My daughter, seated directly behind me, saw the vehicle first and said something like "Whoa, dad!" I looked over my shoulder and saw a blue van skidding and swerving as it tried to avoid slamming into us. It all happened so fast I didn't even have time to react. Luckily the other driver was much more alert than I, and was able to avoid us.

The girls almost immediately resumed their singing, but my heart was pounding as I continued toward the mall. I parked the car and my thumping chest gave way to a sick feeling in my stomach. The girls saw other family members and excitedly hopped out to go meet them. They appeared unfazed, apparently not realizing what had happened. But I knew what had happened. I had almost got my daughter and her friend killed.

Despite having just narrowly avoided the single most tragic event that could happen in my life, when I got home that evening I drank. And because I was on vacation, I drank the next day, and the next. On the fourth day I woke up sick, not hang over sick, but flu-like sick. I lay around that day and had plenty of time to think. I thought mostly about what was happening to my life and what was actually going on with my drinking. I had been thinking specifically about this for several weeks and had to admit that what I now saw was an unmitigated mess. I recognized the ugly truth that if I didn't stop drinking after almost hurting my daughter, I was never going to. I couldn't quit drinking even if I wanted to.

I stayed sick for a couple more days and spent much of the time contemplating life. As 2005 came to an end I arrived at a few unpleasant but purely fact-based conclusions. Though I knew a great deal about recovery and sobriety, I was unable to achieve and maintain it in my own life. Though I hated myself for lying to others about what I was doing, I continued to do so and didn't seem able to stop. Though I was surrounded by people who loved me, hiding my actions from others was causing me to feel the same isolation I had experienced earlier in life.

And lastly, though no one else was aware of it, by separating myself from Christ I was once again adrift spiritually, mired in addiction, and broken in life.

CHAPTER 7

Sixty Second Miracle

I n previous individual chapters I have covered periods as long as five years or more. This chapter will focus generally on a single day and more specifically on a period of about 60 seconds. The significance of this particular minute warrants the greater detail. In order to move forward though, I have to back up a little bit.

One evening about ten days before Christmas that same year, I drove to a nearby city to buy a present for Tracy. On the way home I was listening to the radio and thinking about my life. I wasn't focused on anything too specific, just general concerns about events occurring at the time.

As I drove down the two-lane highway I began to feel something peculiar happening to me as I became less aware of my external environment and much more in tune with my inner-being. It wasn't anything sudden. It was more of a gradual increase in my sensitivity to and awareness of not only what I was thinking about, but also what and who I was. It grew to where I experienced a vivid clarity in my thoughts about life. I felt hyper-alert, connected, and highly energized. Accompanying this powerful awareness was a deep, warm sense of serenity.

The experience lasted just a short time and then ended as gradually as it started when I was distracted by oncoming traffic. I slowly became more aware of what was happening around me and less in tune with the inner-awareness or whatever it was. I remember feeling disappointed when it was gone.

If my description leaves you with only a limited understanding of what I experienced, then you know how I felt. I really didn't know what was happening at the time or what had happened when it was over. I still struggle to put it into words. It was like nothing I had ever experienced before and up to that point, it was one of the most intense feelings of my life. But then it was gone, and I didn't think about it again until a couple of weeks later.

New Year's Eve day did not get off to a good start at our house. My older daughter wanted to go to a party that evening (not an unreasonable request) but Tracy had some concerns about it including location, travel to and from, and people attending (also reasonable concerns). They were having a heated discussion about it, but it was not that big of an issue; that is until I got involved. In a most unreasonable manner I interrupted their discussion and yelled at my daughter for being so argumentative and disrespectful (hypocrisy has been duly noted).

While the situation probably did not warrant its own reality TV show, it was a troubling event. Our home was a long way from perfect, but we didn't make a habit of yelling at each other. This behavior was out of place at our house and was way out of character for me. Afterward I felt terrible and spent most of the day feeling that way.

It wasn't just losing my temper with someone I loved. I knew other things were not right. I knew I wasn't right.

Even though it was a national drinking holiday, I decided early I would not be drinking that day. It had nothing to do with seeking sobriety, I just didn't feel good and had never really been one to enjoy New Years Eve. Over the years I had certainly celebrated and partied (usually considerably more than I should have), but it was more out of obligation than any true celebratory feelings about the day. I hadn't made a New Year's resolution since I was a kid and had always thought the whole thing a particularly insignificant celebration.

Other than the incident with my daughter, the only other memory I have of the afternoon was a strong desire for the entire occasion to just be over with.

That evening after we dropped our younger daughter off at a friend's house, Tracy and I began deciding what to do with ourselves until she would need to be picked up shortly after mid-night. Tracy said there was a club downtown having a dinner with live music. At first I was a little concerned about being around a bunch of alcohol, but I was fairly sure I did not want to drink. We eventually went downtown only to find the event was already finished.

Honestly, I was relieved we had missed it. I knew going into a bar would not have been the best place for me at the time. (Tracy and I still sometimes wonder what would have happened if we would have made it to the event and I ended up drinking.)

Still having several hours to kill, we decided to get something to eat. We went to an Applebee's we frequented and were seated across from the bar. As we waited for our food the thought of having a drink crossed my mind several times but I didn't experience any strong urge to drink. We had been there many times before without drinking and I didn't feel tempted the way I might have been if we had been sitting in a bar.

Due to the large number of patrons and the holiday mood (and drinking), the restaurant was louder than usual. The music playing was barely audible over the din, but at one point I was able to make out one particular song. I had never heard it before but it grabbed my attention, diverting my mind away from the bustling noise of the room. The song (later identified as *Beautiful Wreck*, by Shawn Mullins) produced in me a feeling of deep melancholy or even a profound sadness. But at the same time, I experienced a strong sense of calm, of peacefulness. It was a surprisingly powerful emotional reaction (similar in strength to what one might have to a moving rendition of God Bless America or Amazing Grace), especially considering I was totally unfamiliar with the song. It was actually kind of weird. I mean, it almost made me cry right there in the restaurant.

I didn't mention it to Tracy until we were walking out of the restaurant. I tried to describe the song to her but she did not recall hearing it. When we got to the car I tried to explain how the song had impacted me. She was patient and listened intently, but I soon realized I really didn't know what I was trying to say because I wasn't really sure what had happened. So we changed the discussion to figuring out what to do next.

We reluctantly decided to rent a movie (something we seldom did) and drove to the video store. Looking around at various movies I realized my heart was clearly not in this endeavor. I really just wanted the night to be over with, but I knew I had to stay up at least long enough to pick up my daughter, so getting a movie made practical sense.

After some aimless wandering up and down the aisles of the video store, Tracy called me over to a look at a potential video. It was in the new release section, but the store had stocked only one copy (not exactly a blockbuster). Right there among the many other releases, each with a dozen or more copies on hand, was a single copy of a movie titled *St. Ralph*.

Neither one of us had ever heard of it, but since it was about a teenaged runner and we were both involved in running at the time, we decided to rent it. (Because we loved the movie, we later bought several copies and loaned them out to family and friends. We believed it had a wonderful message and it had special meaning for us. (Interestingly, other than those we have introduced to the movie, we still have never met anyone who has heard of it.)

The movie was about a boy hoping for a miracle cure for

his sick mother. Though a serious subject, it was a lighthearted movie. It was enjoyable but about halfway through I became tired so I lay down on the couch, putting my head on a pillow in Tracy's lap. While there was nothing inherently unusual with this act, it was peculiar in that I had never done it before. I gave it no thought at the time. I was simply tired, so I lay down on the pillow.

◆ ◆ ◆

I soon drifted off to a dreamless, calming, soothing sleep. It was by far the most peaceful slumber of my life.

After only about five minutes, I awoke and told Tracy, "Something weird just happened while I was sleeping."

She asked me what I meant and then listened as I tried to explain, but the best I could come up with was while sleeping, I had felt incredible peace. I hadn't dreamed about peace, I had experienced it. More peace than I had experienced in years, and maybe even in my entire life. Tracy once again heard me out, but just like with the incident involving the song in the restaurant, I was unable to adequately describe what had happened.

I got up just in time to go pick up my daughter and her friend. Driving across town, I thought about how powerful the brief nap had been. These thoughts faded once the girls hopped in the van a little after midnight.

The kids had celebrated New Year's with friends and immediately began to tell me all about their night. We talked nonstop until I pulled off a country road about two miles outside of town and drove up to a farm house where the girls planned to spend the night. After thanking the other girl's mom who had come out to greet us, I said goodnight and backed down the drive way.

As I pulled out onto the road my mind returned to the experience on the couch and I remember wondering what the heck had occurred. I had a feeling even then something unusual was happening or was about to happen, but in a thousand years I would have never guessed what would take place next.

What happened next might be a little hard to believe, but God as my witness (no pun intended) this is exactly what happened.

The straight road had only one stop sign about a half mile from our friend's house. I stopped at the empty intersection and as I accelerated up to the speed limit I began to experience an overwhelming, all-encompassing sensation. It began with the same feeling I had experienced two weeks earlier, but the feeling came on many times stronger; like a hundred times stronger. If the previous experience had provided me with vivid clarity, this time it was an incredibly intense clarity. I have never been so aware or alert. It was as if every bit of doubt, confusion, or uncertainty had utterly vanished from my mind.

This feeling of total clarity was accompanied by the same type of peacefulness I had experienced during my brief nap earlier that evening, but again, many times stronger. I felt completely serene and secure. My entire being, all the way down to my soul, felt as safe as I have ever felt. With brilliant clarity and extraordinary serenity came a feeling best described as a presence, a physical presence. Sitting there in the van I encountered a tangible, palpable presence. I could actually feel it near me, right next to me.

This was not an awareness of the Holy Spirit within me. I had experienced that wonderful feeling before. This was different.

My initial awareness of a physical presence grew until I experienced an awesome sense of knowing. With absolute, concrete certainty, I knew precisely what was happening. I was in the presence of the Lord. He was there and I knowingly accepted his presence. I didn't challenge or question what was occurring. I just allowed it to happen and opened up my entire self to Him.

In the midst of all this, I received the most direct, most

unambiguous, and most important instruction of my life. Without hearing a sound, I received an unmistakable and undeniable message; Jesus Christ told me to stop. With crystal clarity I understood Him to say, "Stop. It's time to stop what you are doing." It was not threatening nor pleading. It came to me purely as a loving statement of fact.

And from that very second I understood His call to me. I knew for certain it was in fact time to stop. I knew right then I was done drinking.

About a mile from the stop sign was a slight bend in the road and when I saw it coming, the acute awareness of the experience began to fade. But even as it did I looked out into the snow-covered field, completely expecting to see Christ standing by the side of the road. Though I didn't see him, I was positive he was there. The intensity of the moment had past, but I never for a minute doubted what I had just experienced was real. And to this day I consider it as real as anything I have ever experienced.

I have come to believe the event was truly timeless in nature, that it took place outside of the constraint of any kind of earthly measurement. But practically speaking, traveling one mile at sixty miles per hour takes about one minute. So this meant the entire experience had lasted only about sixty seconds.

When I got home I told Tracy what happened. This time there was no difficulty in articulating to her what I had been through. I told her I had just been in the presence of God and He had communicated with me. I then told her before going into great detail I wanted to sleep on it and see what my understanding of the event would be in the morning. When I was done speaking I looked in her eyes and saw she believed me. Without hesitation or doubt, through her faith she was able to believe every word I said.

The next morning started as usual with a cup of coffee with Tracy. We talked about the night before and I told her more of my understanding of what happened. I explained I had heard God tell me to change my life. Because she was not aware of the extent of my drinking problem, she wasn't completely sure of what I needed to change, but she was entirely supportive and encouraged me to pursue what I had felt called to do.

I spent the day trying to put together all the events that led up to the experience the night before. I tried to determine if the incident with the song in the restaurant, my nap during the video, and even the drive home from shopping a few weeks earlier were all connected. Though I obviously did not completely understand how God worked, I concluded that in each of these incidents Christ was reaching out for me. But because I had drifted from Him, each time He called I was too focused on earthly concerns or too distracted by worldly noise to hear Him.

Finally, He must have decided I needed a stronger call and it was provided out on that country road. I believed this to be the case then and I still believe it to be the truth today.

Through His call, God had instilled in me a concrete understanding I was to stop drinking and all the nonsense that went with it. The experience also left me with a certainty as to how this was to be accomplished; I would turn my entire life over to Christ. No more trying to hide or separate parts of my life from him. No more trying to do things my way. I would stop pursuing worldly desires and return, just as I had all those years ago in treatment, to listening for God and trusting Him to lead my steps.

That night, as I lay in bed, I thought about what had happened during the last two days. At first it struck me I had woken up a new man, but upon deeper reflection I realized it had not been an overnight conversion. My life had been changed in an instant. Once again, even though I hadn't asked for help, Jesus Christ knew what I needed and had put His open arms around me and saved me from myself.

In my prayers before falling asleep I thanked God for a sober day free of any urges or even thoughts about drinking, the first such day in a long time. I prayed that He would help me stay sober and guide me in all areas of my life. I also asked Him to forgive me for my many sins. Once again I felt connected to Christ. I believed that despite all I had done wrong, despite the fact I had pulled away from Him, God still loved me and had a plan for me. Believing this, I committed myself to doing everything I could to follow His will.

In a brief moment on a cold dark country road I had experienced a miracle. I had received an incredible blessing of which I was totally undeserving. I had received instant healing purely through the grace of Jesus Christ.

And in the following years I would learn that as wonderful as this experience was, what He had planned for the rest of my life was, if not as dramatic, just as amazing.

PART 3
Pursuing God's Call

CHAPTER 8

Seeking to Serve

During the two or three years prior to my experience, I had sworn off alcohol after virtually every drinking episode. But in each instance, often in just a matter of days, I resumed drinking. In the weeks following that night on the country road, this situation finally--and thankfully--changed.

Not only did I not drink alcohol during this time, but I encountered no desire to drink and it seldom even crossed my mind.

As one sober day followed another, it became more and more clear to me that in a brief instant, through His undeserved mercy, God had completely removed my compulsion to drink; and almost as soon as it happened I realized this miracle was about more than just my sobriety. The focus I had lost while drinking suddenly returned, leaving me with a solid understanding of what I was to do with my life. With a strong certainty, I once again believed God intended to use me to help others.

If my past had taught me anything, it was that in order to follow God's call I would have to remain completely sober. I fully believed God had again offered me a life of sobriety, but I also knew I still had the free will to choose whether or not to accept His blessings. Energized by my newfound sobriety, it didn't take me long to decide I was not going to blow this incredible second chance. So I committed myself to doing whatever was necessary to remain sober. I looked at it this way: God had done His part by reopening the door to sobriety and again calling me to serve. Now it was up to me to do the daily work of remaining sober in order to follow the His call. Now it was time for me to do my part.

Deciding where to start this work that would allow me to help others turned out to be rather easy. It was obvious the primary concern would be reconnecting with God, to bridge the gap I had created between us. In order to do this, I made my relationship with Him a much bigger part of my daily life. I increased my daily prayers, asking for the strength to stay sober and the ability to help the men at work. I resumed my pursuit of spiritual growth by reading the Bible and other faith-based literature.

When making daily decisions I listened closely for God's voice and tuned out the noise of the world. And as I gained an understanding of how boastful pride and seeking worldly pleasure had led to my fall, I began practicing humility and truly appreciating the many gifts He had provided.

In reordering my life, the most significant step taken was inviting Christ back into all areas of my life and again relying on His guidance rather than my understanding of how to run my life. Trying to hide parts of my life and living my way had caused me to drift from Him and led me straight back into addiction.

Now, having been given another chance, I turned my entire life back over to Christ and allowed Him back into the driver's seat of our tandem bicycle.

Of course I continued to struggle with sin in my life (as all people do), but I became less ashamed of presenting my life to the Lord. I had read back then we could be made perfect in our relationship with Christ, but the truth was, my worldly behavior was a long way from perfect. So, in attempting to live a life pleasing to God, I set a goal of seeking progress, not obtaining immediate perfection. It had taken me over five years to get so far off track, and I knew attempting to instantly make my entire life right would only lead to disappointment.

So I did my best each day. And although I struggled at times, the good days started to accumulate and with God's help I began to get my life back on track.

◆ ◆ ◆

In contrast to progress I was making in my personal life, the situation at work proved to be more challenging. After time off for the holidays, I had returned to work only to find that although I had undergone a life-changing experience, nothing had changed at the institution.

The truth is jail never really changes. Early in my career an old-timer had told me in his twenty-five years of working in prison virtually nothing had changed, and up to that point in my twenty-plus year career I had seen no significant changes either. Upon my return I found what was generally true for the institution was also true for our treatment program. While I was away the program had not miraculously changed--but I knew I had.

I resumed my job with renewed energy and a strong desire to revitalize what had become a stagnant program. To do this I focused on the part of the program I had the most control over; myself. Examining my part in the decline of the program, I recognized I had made three vital mistakes.

First, I had been distracted by my drinking. Second, I had stopped seeking God's guidance in my work. And my third mistake was accepting (at least partially) the pessimistic notion the program was mostly about men completing treatment just to get an earlier release from custody. There was much work to be done and I knew I would need God's help to do it.

During the following months I prayed my belief in the true value of the program (at least for sincere participants) would be restored. I also prayed for help in my efforts to reinvigorate the program, which included gathering new information, developing new treatment activities, and revamping existing program material.

I attempted to inspire the men by spending more time discussing actual benefits of meaningful treatment and recovery, benefits that went well beyond getting out of jail early. Having once read that good teaching was one part knowledge and three parts theatre, I even tried to be as creative as I could during groups in hopes of increasing the interest of as many men as possible.

Several times I considered reintroducing faith-based principals to treatment (similar to my first group years before) and even sharing my recent life-changing experience. However, I decided against it because I didn't want to infringe on the rights of the men of different faiths. I had spent my career being paid to ensure inmates followed the rules and believed it was important I did the same. Though I still allowed for discussion of spiritual matters in the group, I did not promote any faith system or guide such discussions in any particular direction. If it had been up to me, the entire program would have been overtly spiritual; but it was not up to me.

I continued to do my best to improve the program, but after a while it became clear the prevailing culture (more jail-oriented than recovery-oriented) was not conducive to meaningful treatment. A few guys were being helped and I was thankful for that, but I just wasn't able to bring about the changes I had hoped for. Despite this limited success, I remained committed to trusting God and continued to work hard each day to make the program better.

About a year after my experience, with God's blessing I was still completely sober and excited about what He was doing in my life. Because I had stopped all the nonsense associated with drinking, I was able to be more honest with people I loved and was no longer plagued by the gnawing guilt and shame I had so often felt because of my drinking. I had become closer to God and felt His presence in my daily affairs at work and in my personal life.

It was about this time I decided to expand my effort to serve the Lord. I was still dedicated to the treatment program, but believed I was being called to do more. I prayed that God would guide me toward work beyond what I was doing at the prison and, aided greatly by Tracy, started to pursue other avenues of service.

My first attempt was a great learning experience; that is, I learned one thing I was clearly not meant to do. Tracy and I agreed to co-teach a junior high Sunday school class. To summarize, she was actually quite good at it, I was not.

Tracy next suggested we serve on an adult committee for a local Christian youth group. We worked there for a while with some terrific people, but again, Tracy was much more adept in the role than me. We also helped a wonderful young woman start a faith-based program for at-risk youth, but it was also a poor fit for me. These were all good programs that provided important services. I just did not experience a call to serve in these areas.

While seeking ways to serve the Lord, I had occasionally wondered if sharing the story of my life-altering experience would be an effective way to help others. I knew as Christians we were to tell others of the good Christ had done in our lives. I also knew He had miraculously changed my life for the better and I believed my complete sobriety would be proof enough that something significant had occurred. After considerable thought, I decided to limit my sharing to Tracy, our two girls, and a small number of family members and close friends.

I made this decision for several reasons. First, though I knew exactly what had taken place, I wasn't exactly sure how to accurately explain it to others. Second, in order to tell people what had happened and the significance of it, I would have had to tell them I had again developed a problem with drinking. Most of the people I would have told had no idea I was even drinking and I envisioned the uncomfortable conversation going something like, "Hey guess what? I was saved from my destructive drinking." To which they would reply, "What destructive drinking?"

My belief that boastful pride was part of the nonsense I had been called to eliminate from my life was another reason I didn't share with others. I did not want to be seen as bragging to others, "Look what God did for me. Aren't I something?"

I was hesitant (and remain so even as I write this) to speak about my experience for fear I will come off as boastfully proud. What happened to me was an act of God's grace, not anything for which I can take credit.

The last reason I did not tell others was because I had been around addiction long enough to know how destructive "miracle cures" can be to loved ones when the changes don't last. Addicts often share reports of spontaneous healing with family and friends who, eager for any reason to hope they might get their loved one back, readily accept the addict's story. Thankfully, some of these addicts remain sober and go on to live vastly improved lives. Unfortunately, too many times the instant cure is followed by a relapse, resulting in crushed hopes for all involved.

I wasn't going to share my situation with loved ones until I was sure I wouldn't let them down by drinking again. I believed without question that Jesus Christ had for a second time intervened and saved me. But I also knew I still had free will to choose my behavior. I trusted Him completely. I just didn't yet trust myself.

I always knew someday I would share my story with others. I just wanted to make sure before doing so I had a sound understanding of what actually happened, that sharing it would bring glory to God, and that I was going to be able to maintain lasting sobriety. Until these conditions could be met, I would keep my story mostly to myself.

In the two and a half years following that night on the country road, I had regained significant ground in the ongoing battle between the worldly and the spiritual in my life. By giving God credit for any accomplishments in my life and acknowledging I needed His guidance in all of my daily affairs, I had fought against my natural tendency to be prideful. To counter my desire for worldly pleasure, instead of getting caught up in thinking about various ways to "feel good," I focused on enjoying the wonderful things God was doing in my life. By doing this I remained sober, grew stronger in my faith, and regained hope I could follow the plan God had for me.

That's not to say life was perfect. It has been said into each life a little rain must fall and this time in my life was no exception. In addition to the usual difficulties of family, work, and daily life, I experienced several other more imposing challenges.

I developed a couple of health issues which for the first time in my life limited what I could do physically--not a small deal for an active person. But much more significant than my health concerns was when two of the people I loved most encountered serious, even life-threatening, medical conditions.

The first issue occurred when my younger daughter developed a sever eating disorder. Then a short time later, my mother was diagnosed with cancer. If I had not been able to draw on the strength Jesus Christ provided, either one of these situations likely would have sent me reeling. However, with lots of prayer, God's help, and Tracy's love and support, I stayed on track through both and remained sober.

Looking back I see God had guided me through these hardships and in the process my faith had grown even stronger. The damaging gap between God and I had closed and the God-shaped hole in my heart had healed. I had been broken for a second time in my life when I started drinking again, but even as life continued to present tough challenges, by the grace of God I was being made whole again.

Around this time, on the last day of a treatment group we were having a discussion about the future. Each man was to share what he hoped to be doing in five years. After all the participants had shared, one of the men (a huge guy whose nickname was either a peculiar term of endearment or a scary description of his past behavior) asked what I would be doing in the future. It was an informal discussion so I candidly answered with the truth: I told him I would be doing whatever God called me to do. I added I had been sitting by the phone hoping the Lord would call me to be a professional golfer, but since it didn't look like that was going to happen I would do whatever else He asked of me. We had a good laugh and after dismissing the group for the last time I gave the discussion no additional thought.

Following the completion of the group I took a vacation to enjoy some summer weather. During my time off, I thought about my attempt to restore the program and how I had achieved only limited progress. I also thought about my search for new ways to serve the Lord and admitted I hadn't experienced much success there either. However, rather than being discouraged by these facts, I remained as spiritually motivated and enthusiastic about pursuing God's will as I had ever been.

Though I was trying to practice humility (careful to avoid boastful pride), I couldn't help believing God had big plans for me.

After a week of contemplating what might come next in my life I headed back to work having arrived at two conclusions. The first was that at least for now, I would continue to provide treatment to the men. The second was it was only a matter of time before God would call me away from the institution to something new.

Little did I know I would be wrong on both counts.

The day I returned I walked through the institution just as I had a thousand times before and went directly to my office. You know how certain people who work some place for a long time can tell when something is amiss just by walking into the building? Well, apparently I am not one of those people. Because it

101

was not until late in the morning I became aware that something major had happened at the institution.

Just before lunch I passed by a group room and saw a young lengthy guy leaning on a mop while talking with a big guy who was sitting on a table. I knew the man on the table was not supposed to be in the room so I walked in to tell him to leave. As I entered the room I recognized him as the guy (with the interesting nickname) from my last group. Before I could say anything, the man with the mop asked me, "So what do you think about them moving the females here Mr. Hall?"

Surprised, my only response was an honest, "What are you talking about?"

Together they told me what apparently everyone else in the institution knew: the prison would transition from a male facility to a female facility. The official announcement had been made while I was on vacation.

This change was no small event. In a place where it seems nothing ever changed, this was huge. I stood there dumbfounded and said nothing. Thankfully the guy from my group broke the awkward silence by laughing slightly and saying, "I guess it's like you said Mr. Hall."

"How's that?" I replied, still processing the news.

"God must want you to work with the females," he answered. "You remember telling us that you would do whatever He called you to do. Well, this must be it."

I thought for a second and said, "I guess you could be right." I left the room, completely forgetting to tell the big guy to leave, and headed back to my office.

Over the next few days I learned the details of the coming transition. Though the idea of such a major change caused justified concern for some people, after I got over the initial shock, I was actually excited about what was happening. I had been praying for new ways to serve God and was now being given the opportunity to do new work right where I was. I considered the transition a blessing and knew God would guide me through the challenges which lay ahead.

During the next few months the men were transferred from the institution. Before they had all left, I had one final conversation with a former program participant; a conversation which I have always believed served as a fitting end to this part of my career.

The former participant was a rough, biker-type guy but a good rapport had developed between us. The day he came to see me he started by thanking me for helping him change his life. He told me he had been in and out of jail and addicted to drugs since he was a kid. He said he never thought his life would change and admitted he had only entered treatment to get some time off his sentence. He became emotional as he went on to tell me that during the program I had given him hope for a better future. He was clearly not used to showing emotion around others but, through the slightest of tears, he continued. He said he had two adult children at home who were struggling with addiction and he now believed he would have the chance to help them as a real father should. He finished by thanking me again for helping him become a better man.

I could tell he was feeling uncomfortable and he looked ready to leave, so I quickly wished him well, encouraged him to keep working hard, and thanked him for the kind words. What I didn't have time to tell him before he left was what I fully understood to be the truth: It was not me who deserved his thanks. I was merely an instrument. The thanks belonged to God.

Three years into my new found sobriety, my ten-plus years of working with men were over. Though I would receive no official special recognition for my work, I had received something much more meaningful. I had seen a man who once thought he was destined to a life of addiction, pain, and prison express heartfelt gratitude for what he had received in my program. Working through me, God had given this lost man real hope that life could be better. And it was awesome to have played a small part in this.

CHAPTER 9

Admission to Brokenness

W omen began arriving in late fall of 2008 but with the entire institution in a state of flux it was going to be awhile before any substantial programming, including drug treatment, would be offered. Recognizing the women needed something to do (boredom probably causes as many problems in prison as anything else) I decided to facilitate a public speaking group. I'd had some success with a few such groups with men and thought it would be a good way to get women involved in something productive. I found a space on one of the living units, got a few women signed up and planned a starting date.

The group met the first day in a dank TV room with sheet metal shoddily welded over all the windows. With mismatched tables and chairs, terrible acoustics, poor lighting, and a rather unpleasant odor, it had to be the worst room I had ever worked in. Resources were scarce, so for a lectern we used a rickety old ironing board. (The next week, someone had stolen the ironing board so we had to use a big trash can.) The group started out fine and I remember thinking that it was going to be kind of fun working with women. Then we took a break.

During the break (the first break of the first group I ever facilitated with women), I stepped into the hallway for a drink but before making it to the water fountain I was hastily approached by a very large, tough looking woman from the group. She walked right up to me (a lot closer than I was used to having an inmate stand) and got about three words out before bursting into tears. As she stood there sobbing in obvious anguish, she tried to tell me she needed help and wanted to talk to me (me?) about her problems. I was caught off guard by how distraught she was and though I don't remember exactly what I said to her, it helped enough that she was able to return to the group after the break.

Walking back to my office after the group I felt a little unsure of myself and wondered how I was going to work with such emotional and hurting people? Men had of course experienced pain in their lives, but they rarely, if ever, demonstrated their feelings so openly. I realized right then working with female inmates was going to be very different.

Over the next couple of days I thought about my prayers asking God to call me to something new, and I have to admit the old expression "be careful what you ask for" crossed my mind a few times. But in the following weeks, as I continued to pray for strength, I became much surer of myself and of the Lord's hand in what was happening. Instead of worrying about how I (in my own ability) was going to help these hurting women, I held fast to my faith and trusted that God would guide me in this new work.

As we prepared for the transition to female participants, we learned we would also be changing the type of treatment we provided. In this new mode of treatment, rather than working with just one group for the duration of their treatment (while other staff in my position did the same with their own groups), I would work with every group in the program during at least a portion of their treatment. Working with every woman at some point in their program would require me to provide treatment to many more participants than I had in the past.

In addition to this structural change, there was a philosophical change which would require my role to transform from one of teaching participants about recovery (which I loved) to one in which I provided therapy (which I did not love) to promote recovery. In short, I was to change from being a teacher to functioning as a therapist. I had embraced the transition to female participants, but I was extremely reluctant to embrace these two additional changes.

I believed God was directing my steps in life, but there was still a part of me that wanted to do things my way. And sharing groups with other staff and a more therapeutic approach were not "my way."

Despite my strong reservations, once it became clear the changes were inevitable, I knew I needed to get ready for working with women in this new style of treatment. I read numerous books and articles on the subject and of the many insights gleaned from these sources, the most important was the idea that effective treatment for women needed to be tailored specifically to their needs. This meant I would not be able to simply present the program to women as I had to male participants. Instead, I would need to make major changes to what I presented and how I presented it.

To learn more about these changes and how to make them, I attended various training events which addressed my role in our new program and provided specific strategies for working with female participants. Much of the training was helpful and during my early work with women I used a good amount of the information provided at these events. But what stuck with me most was a brief interaction I had with a psychologist who during the previous three days of training had learned I was the only male staff member in our program.

This doctor, who had spent years working with female offenders, pulled me aside and started by telling me that due to my physical appearance and demeanor I would likely remind many women of their fathers. This comment came as no great surprise to me. You see, I didn't (and still don't) look much like a typical drug counselor or therapist. In fact, do you remember that kid in your neighborhood whose dad was a tall skinny guy with a crew cut who seemed to wear the same white shirt every day and looked perpetually angry? Well, I look just like that kid's dad.

The second thing the doctor told me, the thing he was much more emphatic about, caught me a little more off guard. He said because I would remind women of their fathers or other males who had treated them poorly in the past, many would transfer their hatred of these other men to me.

I was surprised by how he said this, as if it was simply an undeniable or unavoidable fact. He had essentially said, "The women will hate you. That's all there is to it!"

I had arrived at this particular training knowing women would need a great deal of help and some would have a hard time trusting a male facilitator. I left having been told in addition to these two considerable challenges, there was a good chance (at least according to one experienced psychologist) many women would hate me even as I tried to help them. It was becoming increasingly clear working with female participants was going to be a formidable challenge.

After a few months of preparation, training, and daily prayers for guidance, I started our first drug treatment group consisting of women. In the initial weeks of this and every subsequent group, I was required to conduct interviews with each participant, just as I had with men. Before each interview, to gather background information I always read the Pre-sentencing Investigation report (a report detailing much of the individual's history). Many of the men's reports had included personal histories of abuse and neglect, but I was shocked by how many women's read like real-life horror stories.

I won't go into specifics here (and really, if you grew up

with a fairly normal life, you probably wouldn't believe me anyway), but these reports detailed some of the most horrendous abuse and dysfunctional lives imaginable.

When the interviews started I encountered the saddest life stories I had ever heard and, as hard as it was to believe, it seemed each women's story was worse than the one before.

Reading the women's histories had provided only part of the picture; listening to their stories allowed me to gain a deeper understanding of all they had experienced. Though many women initially presented a tough exterior (a common mask worn in prison), most eventually broke down and revealed their true feelings. Their pain, despair, and shame were clearly evident as they cried through their stories.

One after another, I encountered women who had been systematically neglected, abused, and traumatized--many for their entire lives--not only by strangers, but more tragically by the very people who were supposed to love and protect them. Some had seen terrible insult added to tragic injury when their families turned against them, and even blamed them, when the women finally reported sexual abuse. Many participants had been abused as children and then again in intimate relationships as adults.

Sadly, not a small number carried visible physical scars from past abuse. There seemed to be no limit to the depths of depravation, degradation, and torment to which these women had been subjected.

I had come across plenty of terrible stories in my work as a guard and again while writing Pre-sentencing reports (my supervisor used to assign me the worst cases specifically because of my past experience), but my focus had always been on the perpetrators of heinous acts, not the victims. It did not take long before it became clear I simply was not professionally prepared for dealing with people who had been victimized as these women had.

As I struggled through the initial interviews, at times I considered remaining completely removed from the powerful emotions women experienced while sharing their stories.

I could have easily done this. Years earlier, after encountering the little boy disfigured by his mother, I had nearly perfected the ability to remain dispassionate around inmates, particularly female inmates. But I knew this was not what these women needed. They needed to know someone cared enough to truly listen to them, to be emotionally present with them. I had been called to help these women and knew I wouldn't be able to do so if I remained emotionally distant.

Knowing I would need help in this endeavor, Tracy and I began to pray that I might receive strength and guidance in meeting women in their pain. Thankfully, God answered our prayers and I was able to conduct the interviews in a compassionate and effective manner.

Looking back, I realize that while the hurt evident in the woman during my first public speaking group had afforded an initial glimpse into the immense pain women carried, it was these early interviews that provided a thorough introduction to a world of brokenness I never knew existed. Though I knew not everything I had been told was true (yes, occasionally people in jail lie), I concluded if even half of it was, many of these women were in great need of help.

Throughout the first year I continued to learn valuable lessons about working with female participants. I figured out right away that just like some men, there were women who had absolutely no interest in changing their lives; they simply wanted time off their sentence. They were committed to criminal lifestyles and had every intention of remaining that way. These individuals hindered attempts to develop a healthy treatment environment and directly interfered with those women making honest attempts at recovery.

Unfortunately, by offering a shorter sentence for completing the program, we attracted inmates who were neither ready for treatment nor, in some cases, even remotely interested in change. I understood this just came with the territory, but it was and remained one of the most distracting and discouraging aspects of my work.

Much more encouraging than learning about a small number of completely uninterested participants was finding out there were many women who had a genuine <u>desire to change</u>. In fact, the number of female participants sincerely interested in recovery was <u>much higher</u> than with men. Of the numerous reasons for this, the most easily identifiable was women's desire to be involved in their <u>children's lives.</u> Many of these participants honestly wanted to be better mothers than they had been in the past and realized if they continued to abuse drugs they would never be able to do so. Working with motivated participants made parts of my job easier and made the entire process much more meaningful.

One of the more disheartening findings was learning the women's brokenness extended beyond the awful scars of past physical abuse. Many suffered from a more subtle but just as painful brokenness. These women struggled with the agonizing question of why they had not been loved or cared for by their mothers, and in too many cases the even more troubling question of why they themselves had failed to properly love and care for their own children.

Discussions of these two issues brought out more anguished tears than any other topic. Some women, even those honestly working toward recovery, were never able to directly confront these particular concerns; it was just too painful.

Discussions about fathers came up less frequently; but when they did it was almost as sad as discussions about mothers. The unfortunate refrain, "I never really knew my real dad" was far too common. And as the women shared their life stories, it became clear many had never experienced a healthy father figure while growing up and had even worse luck in finding a healthy male in adult relationships. Instead, many had been subjected to the worst the male gender had to offer. Whether it was due to an absent or cruel father, another abusive male figure while growing up, or abusive male partners in their intimate relationships (or all of the above), the absence of any healthy males in their lives--for some, their entire life--was another piece of their brokenness.

Certainly not all women had been abused or felt unloved by their families. But as is generally true for women in any prison our participants received much less family support than their male counterparts.

For instance, women generally get fewer visits than males, with many women getting no visits at all. (We once asked a group of over 100 participants if they had received a visit in the last year and only about 20 raised their hands. This number would have been much higher had we asked the men.) The most basic explanation for this is that when a man goes to prison his mom or girlfriend visits him (often bringing his kids), but when a women goes to prison the men in her life seldom visit and her family is often unwilling or unable to do so, sometimes because they are too busy taking care of the inmate's children. In addition to the limited visits, it is also common to hear women speak of writing countless letters home to family, including their children, only to have the letters go unanswered for months at a time.

The neglect experienced by these women goes beyond their families. Women in prison are mostly unknown to people in our society (though this is changing somewhat due to popular TV shows about women in prison). When our prison transitioned to females and I told people in the community the institution would eventually house over a thousand inmates, almost without exception they asked, "Where in the world would you get that many female inmates?"

This was a reasonable response as most people understandably give little thought to incarcerated females. Though they are currently the fastest growing group of inmates in America, other than limited notice received from the above mentioned exploitative cable shows, they remain a group of mostly ignored and forgotten people. (By the way, we had no problem filling the institution.)

❖ ❖ ❖

Work in those early groups revealed that of the women who had thankfully escaped any past physical or emotional abuse, a large number had unfortunately engaged in terribly self-destructive behavior while pursuing their addiction. (Sadly, a majority of women had experienced both.) These women described lives in which one bad decision was followed by several even worse ones. The most damaging decision reported by many was when they choose to push away loved ones who were willing to help and turned instead to drugs and people (usually older men) who really did not care for them.

The immense shame women felt for what others had done to them was often equaled, and sometimes even surpassed, by the enormous guilt they carried for what they themselves had done.

While a few were remorseful about their criminal behavior (almost always related to their drug use), what haunted many more was the repeated compromising of their morals and a failure to fulfill their most basic responsibilities in life. Some women had sold or traded their bodies for drugs, and many had remained in appallingly dysfunctional relationships in order to maintain a steady supply of drugs. Some had lost children to social services, while others who still had kids had severely damaged their relationships by failing to adequately care for them.

Considering all the women had been through--and I've provided only a partial description of what they reportedly experienced--it made perfect sense when group work revealed that in addition to shame and guilt, many suffered from extremely low self-worth and possessed little if any self-confidence. As concerning as these traits were, the most troubling characteristic I saw in women was a deep sense of hopelessness. Too many had simply given up hope that life could get better.

By the end of the first year it was clear that in being called to help this group of hurting people, I had been presented with a daunting task. However, rather than shying away from the challenge, I continued to pray to God each day for guidance and thanked Him for the tremendous opportunity.

It has been said when responding to God's call the key is availability, not ability. This was certainly the case with me. I may not have had all the required skills, but I had total faith that if I made myself available--that is, remained willing to do whatever I was called to do--God would provide the strength I needed to complete the work He had set before me. And the more I worked with female participants, the surer I became I was where God wanted me. I recognized that despite their brokenness, there were many women still willing to fight for their lives. I knew a little about brokenness and wholeheartedly believed Jesus Christ had saved me from mine in order to help this group of women rise up out of theirs.

CHAPTER 10

Instrument of Restoration

T he beginning of my second year was marked by the completion of our first treatment group. Twenty women who had lived, worked, and grown together for almost an entire year successfully completed the program. The group had gone surprisingly well and a good number of participants had benefited from the experience. There had of course been challenges along the way, including establishing group rules and norms, creating a healthy environment, and, my biggest hurdle, developing a more therapeutic approach to facilitating the program. But even considering these and other difficulties that arose along the way, it would be fair to say from the very beginning good things were happening in the program.

As we moved into the second year, the program began to function even more effectively and I started to see more women sincerely engage in treatment and make significant positive changes in their lives.

I witnessed women who had previously sabotaged their lives with poor choices begin to make self-enhancing decisions that helped them move toward newly established life goals. Others did admirable work toward forgiveness--one of the most significant components of recovery. They began to forgive others and, more importantly, forgive themselves. Forgiving others allowed them to let go of resentments which had kept them stuck in the past, while forgiving themselves (or at least beginning to) provided relief from the crushing shame and guilt so many carried with them.

hope → responsibility

I saw participants gain an understanding of their addiction and actually believe, some for the first time, that sobriety was a viable option in their lives. They took full responsibility for their actions and recognized if they were responsible for creating a drug-abusing lifestyle in the past, they could be responsible for creating a drug-free lifestyle in the future. Many women were helped by examining past unhealthy relationships and learning not only what a healthy relationship looked like, but also that they deserved to have such relationships in their lives.

Of course not every participant benefited from the program, but this was no surprise considering that some had entered treatment with no intention of changing. Still, for every woman who remained unchanged there were several who were deeply impacted by their work.

In no area was this impact more evident than in how participants viewed themselves. Many, who in the past had been told repeatedly that what they had to say did not matter, came to believe their thoughts and opinions were as valuable as anyone else's. Women who entered treatment feeling lost and worthless were able to regain a sense of who they really were. By challenging their deeply held negative beliefs about themselves, many began to see that despite the mistakes they had made they were still decent people worthy of meaningful lives.

And as they began to feel better about themselves, they developed confidence to take on challenges of recovery and the hope that life could be better.

In many cases, improved self-concept went beyond internal emotional healing and growth. There were women who actually underwent a sort of physical transformation. I am not talking about altering their hair, changing their make-up, or losing weight; these women literally looked (and acted) like different, healthier people as a result of their work in treatment. Many who initially walked around with their heads down, avoided eye contact and were reluctant to even speak to others, learned to stand up straight, engage people face to face, and assertively speak their minds.

As subsequent groups completed our program and women were released from custody, I was confident they would be leaving in a good position to be successful in life. In time this proved to be true as the number of former participants returning to prison (the most obvious indicator of failure) remained low and the number of women reportedly doing well was encouragingly high.

Sadly, we received reports of women relapsing, with tragic results in a couple of cases. But we received many more stories of women who had left prison and began creating the meaningful lives they deserved. These women became employed, enrolled in school, participated in support groups, developed healthy relationships and took an active role in their children's lives.

In describing all these life-altering changes, I'm not suggesting they all occurred solely as a result of participants working with me or that every woman in the program was helped by my efforts. The participants benefited from their work with other staff and were also helped immensely from work with peers who provided support, encouragement, constructive feedback, caring advice, and a sense of belonging. Interaction among participants was the foundation of our mode of treatment and the component of the program from which many women benefited the most. Without question some women were helped more by other aspects of the program than they were by working with me.

There were, however, a significant number of women who made the type of progress described above (and grew in other ways) as a direct result of their work in my groups. I know this because I witnessed it first hand and, much more significantly, because women told me themselves.

These were the women I believed God called me to help.

Having already stated I was not responsible for all the positive changes women experienced, it's important to make clear I don't even believe I was responsible for benefits they experienced directly from their work with me. To a great degree, I believe the wonderful changes I witnessed actually occurred in spite of me--at least in spite of the worldly me.

Up to the time I started working with women (and even more so before I started working with men), I had always tended to be impatient, judgmental, opinionated, critical of others, and very set in my ways. I was self-centered, emotionally reserved, and generally not a very approachable person. I had little interest in relationships outside of my family and a few close friends, and had never been overly concerned with other people's problems. In addition to these personal traits, early in my career I had become dispassionate, unsympathetic, and even hateful and abusive toward inmates.

Many of these characteristics had served me well while I was a guard and though Christ had changed me in some ways during my work in treatment with men (such as removing the hatred from my heart to allow a good rapport to develop), most of these traits remained intact and didn't cause any major problems.

In fact, male participants had responded quite well to these traits. They enjoyed the brisk pace of daily activities, appreciated my sincere but business-like approach, and understood constructive criticism. Of course it helped that the men were not terribly interested in exploring deep emotional issues and were mostly content to deal with their own problems. This meant I did not need to possess the personal traits or professional skills required to deal with such difficult issues.

However, the situation was vastly different with women. With them everything was about relationships and emotions. They had a strong desire to talk about their problems and needed a great deal of time to process their feelings. Many female participants feared being judged and most did not respond well to direct or harsh criticism. In general, they required a more patient, caring, and understanding approach to treatment. Taking these factors into consideration, the negative traits I possessed and my lack of therapeutic skills (not to mention my dislike of female inmates) made me a highly unlikely candidate for working successfully in a therapeutic program for female participants.

All these factors make what happened in my work with women more amazing. If it had been a case of a highly skilled therapist or some altruistic natural born do-gooder helping the women, I don't think it would have been as noteworthy. But for someone like me to have been effective in our program was truly remarkable. That I was able to help these women make meaningful changes in their lives served as proof that God had not only guided me in my work, but had also changed me in the process.

The bottom line is that without the helping and shaping hand of God, the worldly me simply would not have been successful in this particular program.

Of the many ways I recognized God's hand in my work, probably the first was when my grave concern about women's hatred of me interfering with treatment proved to be completely unwarranted. I encountered no such animosity and honestly don't recall a single female participant who struggled due to transferring their hatred of other males to me. (Plenty women disliked me at times, but it wasn't because of their feelings toward other males, it was because I held them strictly accountable for their behavior.)

The fact was, instead of encountering women who were blocked by subconscious or pre-determined hatred of me, I encountered women who responded remarkably well to interactions with me.

Maybe the most meaningful example of women responding positively to my work with them was the level of trust that developed between us. Though some were at first understandably hesitant to open up around a man, in just a short time the majority began to share significant personal issues with me.

I was actually surprised at the high level of trust women displayed and some of them were too. When we discussed the issue of trust, many participants reported that although they weren't sure why, what they shared with me and what they shared in group discussions while I was present was more than they had ever before shared around a man.

To help build trust, I created an atmosphere where it was safe for women to be themselves. I did this by first describing the masks addicts hide behind and then suggesting they remove any they might have once used or were currently using. Most readily acknowledged they wore such masks, but some were hesitant to remove theirs because they knew the masks kept others at a distant. After years of being burned by trusting others and letting them get too close, it made sense these women were leery about letting anyone see the real person behind the mask.

To encourage them, I tried to share the "real" me to a much greater degree than I had with the men. Though it went against my nature, letting women see that I too struggled at times and was affected by life's emotional ups and downs seemed to help them believe it was safe to share their real selves with the group. When they were courageous enough to do so, I responded by accepting them just as they were. I believed that encountering a non-judgmental person would help women develop enough trust to share their authentic selves. In many cases this proved to be true and of all the participants I worked with, those who benefited most were the ones who trusted enough to work on their real selves.

Though I had been warned by a well-intentioned doctor that female participants would dislike and distrust a male counselor, I experienced no such problems.

While I couldn't be completely sure of God's role in the women's response to me, I was absolutely sure that left to my own devices I would have never acted in ways that allowed women to feel so comfortable trusting me. I was convinced that of all the reasons God called me to work with women, one of the most important was to provide a male figure they could trust. And the fact I was able to interact in such an open and non-judgmental way was a powerful indication God was indeed changing me.

◆ ◆ ◆

Another important way God's hand was evident in my work was how He moved me to become more patient with female participants. One of the earliest examples of this occurred one morning when an older woman who had clearly traveled a rough road in life approached me and asked, "Mr. Hall, do you remember yesterday when you told our group what I had said during a discussion last week?"

As I nodded my head yes, she began to cry. With big tears streaming down her face, she told me, "That was the first time in my life a man listened to me and cared enough to remember what I had to say."

If I had been racing along at my normal worldly pace I could have easily missed what she had said, and even if I had heard it I might not have cared enough to remember it. Instead, I had truly listened to her and understood what she had to say and, judging by her reaction as she stood there sobbing, it had been a significant event for her. When she completed the program several months later she again thanked me for listening to her, saying it helped her believe what she had to say was important. She added that being listened to by someone who really cared helped her believe *she* was important.

I already knew from personal experience it was important for recovering people, especially those beaten down by life, to gain a sense of significance in their life. But it wasn't until I saw how powerfully this woman was impacted that I realized this could be at least partially accomplished by simply slowing down and really listening to participants. When I did this, women responded well and many who had arrived at treatment having effectively lost their voice in life began to believe what they had to say really mattered.

To witness a woman who had been told for years to be quiet (or much worse) believe in herself enough to speak up--knowing she deserved to be heard--was one of the most rewarding parts of my work.

One such participant was a petite woman who early in treatment was almost removed from the program due to lack of participation. Fortunately, she remained and as she began to discuss her past I learned her quietness was not due to a lack of desire to change. Her reluctance to participate was the result of being repeatedly told by men in her life nobody cared about what she had to say. Realizing this, I did my best to show her she had the right to share her thoughts and that others cared enough to listen. This work continued for several months until she was called into my office after missing a required meeting.

When she arrived at my office I immediately began to reprimand her. Suddenly, she interrupted me and said, "Mr. Hall, I couldn't make it to the meeting yesterday. I had another appointment and couldn't possibly have kept both."

I was a taken aback by being interrupted, but rather than getting angry (my natural response) I felt so proud of her I could barely keep the smile from my face. Early in treatment this woman had lacked the self-confidence to even engage in private conversation with her peers. Now, here she was boldly standing up for herself. It was a beautiful thing. I told her how proud she should be for being so assertive and I could tell she felt good about herself as she left. I saw that pride again the next day when I praised her in front of the entire treatment community.

Though I felt the Lord's presence in my work each day, I still encountered trying circumstances. Ironically, one of the most difficult issues was establishing the proper role of spirituality in our program.

The women often talked about their faith and the positive impact it was having on their recovery, and I never hid the significant part my faith played in my recovery. But because we were still operating under the same guidelines (requiring that the program refrain from promoting any particular faith) every time the subject came up I had to decide how much sharing should be allowed and sometimes had to limit the spiritual nature of activities or presentations.

For instance, on certain days women would sing together during our morning gathering and one day the chosen music was a Christian song. Well, I knew we couldn't have women singing what amounted to a Sunday school song at our meeting, especially since everyone present was required to participate in the activity. We had women of other faiths and others who did not subscribe to any faith-based world view and their rights had to be protected. So I stopped the singing.

The next day several women approached me saying they were concerned I was prohibiting them from practicing spirituality as part of their treatment. This situation and others like it left me in the challenging and uncomfortable position of feeling like I was discouraging women from faith-based recovery.

Of course, nothing could be further from my beliefs about their sobriety. In their brokenness, I believed there was nothing they needed more than to accept Jesus Christ and trust Him to guide their lives. That's what made this situation so difficult; I felt like I was minimizing the importance of spirituality to a group of people who would benefit most from a faith-based approach to recovery. I prayed about this often and trusted that the Lord was guiding me to do the right thing, but at times it still felt like I was trying to help the women with one hand tied behind my back.

The role of spirituality in our program may have been

limited, but there was nothing prohibiting me from promoting the second part of my old motto: trust God and work hard. It was here in my approach to encouraging hard work and providing genuine encouragement that I witnessed another example of God changing me in order to reach more of the women.

During my work with the men I had always encouraged them to work hard, but honestly, when it became clear that a man was not interested in treatment I quickly shifted my energy to those who were. It was different with the women. With them I experienced a strong calling to be persistent in pushing all to work hard, including the uncommitted and difficult to reach women. When I noticed a woman begin to disengage, rather than just ignoring the situation (as I might have with a male participant) I confronted them by explaining the expectation was that everyone, including them, would work hard every day.

As insistent as I was in demanding that the women work hard, I was just as persistent in providing encouragement to do so. I repeatedly told them regardless of how far down they had fallen, if they were willing to work hard each day, I truly believed they could get back up again. I told them, "If I can do it, I believe you can do it."

This simple concept, telling women I believed in them, gave many hope for a better future. I remembered from my time in treatment that it was gaining hope that had allowed me to begin to see myself as worthy and capable of a better life, and I began to see the same thing happening with the women. When they learned someone truly believed in them, it not only provided increased optimism for the future (hope), but also produced a positive change in how they viewed themselves. And, for some, this proved to be a big, even life-changing step forward.

The powerful impact of being believed in was evident at a morning gathering one day when an entire group nearing the end of the program stood in front of the full auditorium. Each woman was to describe the most important lesson they would take from their experience in treatment. After several participants had shared, they came to a small woman who spoke with a strong accent. Though this woman had been reluctant to participate early on, I had repeatedly provided her with stern, but genuine encouragement. In time, she became an active participant who benefited greatly from treatment.

When it was her turn to speak she said, "The most important thing I got out of treatment was having Mr. Hall say that he believed in me."

Crying, she continued, "In all my life I have never had anyone say they believed in me. I know he really means it. And now I believe in myself."

Because God had guided me in becoming more persistent in encouraging hard-to-reach participants, this woman (along with others just like her) was able to finally receive a message that helped her see her future, and herself, in a more hopeful way.

Sometimes God's direct presence in my work manifested itself in more lighthearted ways. An example of this was when a participant would tell me at the end of treatment that something I said had been so inspiring and had so directly spoken to their needs that it had changed their lives.

This was wonderful to hear, but the thing was, many times the words they quoted were words I had never spoken! And this happened a lot. I would thank them for the expression of gratitude, all the while smiling inside knowing they received what they needed; they had heard what they needed to hear, not from me, but from God speaking through me.

Whether serious or light-hearted, the best single illustrations of how God worked through me was in a special group I started about two years into the new program. This particular four week group brought about the most profound results of any work in my entire career and right from its inception I knew God was guiding me.

I got the idea for the group from Tracy (seems like lots of great things in my life began with her) after she read an article about a group of men who gathered regularly to listen to each other's stories. No discussion afterward, just sharing a story while other people listen. I read a little more about it and recognized such a process would fill a need in our treatment program.

The issue was, when women shared personal experiences in our groups they were almost always provided with feedback from their peers. For as long as I had been doing groups, I had suspected there were experiences women might have wanted to share but declined to do so because they were apprehensive about the feedback they might receive (i.e., being criticized, judged harshly, or even patronized). Believing it could be helpful, I decided to create a group where women could share personal life experiences without receiving any feedback; just simply sharing their story, to hear it out loud, to get it off their chests.

As soon as I started putting the ideas together I felt a surge of energy and knew something special was happening.

When the group started, my initial assumptions were immediately proven right; women had plenty of stories they wanted to share in this particular forum. The group began with eight pre-screened women and over four sessions each woman shared twice, choosing their own topics. The experiences they shared included instances of severe trauma, crushing tragedy, and utter heartbreak. Though the groups were more difficult and emotionally painful (for all involved) than any group I had ever been a part of, I never doubted the Lord was present. I often prayed silently for women after they shared and felt God's healing power in the room.

I can't explain it and don't even fully understand it, but the results of the initial sessions and subsequent groups were nothing short of incredible. Virtually every woman reported being positively affected by the experience. Some said they finally felt "unstuck," even after having been stuck for many years. Others said a huge burden had been lifted, that they felt less shame and were more able to forgive others and themselves. Several, who had previously struggled to make much progress in treatment, suggested the group provided a boost to their motivation toward recovery and their subsequent work indicated they had indeed undergone a striking change. A good number stated emphatically that the group had changed their lives, and more than a few even suggested it had played a big part in saving theirs.

After facilitating a couple of these groups, I came across the phrase, "a wound needs oxygen to heal". Just a short time later, I read someplace that the reason we work to heal our past wounds is so we can stop bleeding on our present. I immediately thought, that's what is happening with the women in my group.

The women in the group had grown tired of their past hindering their present and had finally decided to get out in the open their troubling experiences, to expose them to clean air, to let them go, and to allow for healing to begin. In every group I witnessed amazing occurrences as once-wounded women took bold steps to begin the extremely difficult process of healing. Each time we met I was struck by their courage, and every time we met I told them so.

This particular program, one in which I saw more profound change than any other I had ever facilitated, was totally separate from our program curriculum. It was something I developed and would not have existed if not for me. I mention this not to boast but rather to point out the most important aspect of all this: If God hadn't changed my heart I would have never started a group that required me to go even deeper into the women's problems and pains. If He wouldn't have moved me in ways that allowed the women to trust me, they would have never participated in a group that required so much exposure and vulnerability.

Even more fundamentally than this, if Jesus Christ hadn't saved me from my addiction, I would not have been there at all.

These are the plain facts: without me, there would have

been no such group, but without Christ's awesome grace, there would have been no me. For this reason all credit for this life-changing group, and for every other benefit the women received from any of my work, goes directly to the Lord.

Truly, in all that I've described in this writing, all thanks go to God. For there simply would be no me without Him.

At the end of each treatment group, a completion ceremony was held to commemorate the women's achievements in the program. They had worked hard and it was important they received special recognition for their effort. Members of the completing group were responsible for developing the program and a great deal of work went into this preparation. Administrators, staff from various departments, and other program participants crowded into the auditorium for each of these events. In the small world of prison drug treatment, these ceremonies were a big deal.

As a part of each of these events, one of the completing women would read a prepared thank you to each treatment staff member. I was always struck by what they mentioned, or really, what they didn't mention, when it came to my turn. They almost never said thanks for teaching them how to think more rationally, communicate better, manage their anger more effectively, or avoid relapse (all important components of recovery which we spent long hours processing). Instead, stating that these helped them most in changing their lives, they invariably thanked me for the same three things; treating them decently, believing in them, and giving them hope.

It was not uncommon for the woman speaking to become emotional while expressing her gratitude to me, and I always felt more than a little uncomfortable receiving such heartfelt praise in front of a crowded auditorium. Of course it was nice to hear, but I knew the thanks went to God. I sat (and at times squirmed) through about a dozen of these events before one group finally got it right. And when they did, it wasn't only the best completion event I had ever attended; it was the best day I ever had at work.

    It began on the last day of this particular group when one of the participants asked to speak with me. This woman had arrived at treatment having basically given up on life. She had lost her children and stated she had no intention of trying to get them back. She was plagued with such self-loathing and feelings of worthlessness that she considered herself undeserving of recovery or even a decent life. And she was filled with a strong hatred (which she made no attempt to conceal) that drove away almost anyone she encountered.

    These unpleasant traits became completely understandable when, early in my work with her, I learned of her background. Hers was a history full of repeated instances of extreme neglect, heartbreaking loss, and unspeakable abuse. In fact, this woman had as rough a history as any inmate I had ever encountered in my thirty-year career.

    Yet, despite her incredibly negative self-concept and off-putting behavior, I knew there was a part of her that wanted, and deserved, help. I decided to look beyond her disagreeable personality and committed myself to helping her just as I would any other participant. Though her progress in treatment would be slow, in what I considered an amazing turn of events she ultimately did quite well in the program and made meaningful strides toward changing her life for the better.

    When we met after group that last day she began by smiling and thanking me, but then became deadly serious and said, "I tried to hate you when we started treatment."

    I remembered our initial encounters and said, "I know you did."

    Beginning to cry, she went on, "But I couldn't hate you because I knew you wanted to help me."

    I nodded my head again.

Crying even harder she said, "You changed my life Mr. Hall ... You saved my life."

I was moved by her words and thanked her, then began to gently correct her by saying that God had changed her life. But as I was talking she was overcome with emotion and walked away. Though she was unable to respond, I hoped she had heard and understood me.

A couple days later the same woman spoke at the group's completion event. Standing at the front of the auditorium, she talked about her peers, thanked the other staff involved with the program, then turned toward me, seated to the left of the podium, and immediately started crying.

She composed herself enough to begin, "Mr. Hall you treated us like people. You believed in us and you gave us hope."

Again she began to cry, as did several other members of her group seated to the right of the podium, facing the audience. I saw all this happening and, fearing things were falling apart, considered intervening.

But before I could, she pulled herself together and shakily began again, "Mr. Hall ... we thank God for you and for putting you in our lives ...."

I don't remember everything else she said, but I do remember how happy I was that I let her finish. Because she had finally, publicly, said what should have been said every time a participant thanked me for my work; it wasn't me who deserved thanks. It was the Lord.

In considering all the ways God worked in my life during my time with the women, what stands out most is how resistant I had initially been to the structural changes and the more therapeutic approach to treatment in our new program. I thought I knew exactly what I needed in order to be successful in helping others, but it turned out He had a much better idea of what would be best.

I soon learned it was these very changes that would allow me to work with more women at a much deeper, more meaningful level. Once I had recognized this was all part of God's plan, I committed myself to following His will and trusting Him to guide me in my work. And to this day, He has done just that, with some amazing results.

◆ ◆ ◆

I started by saying I was inspired to write this story after reading a simple phrase in a daily devotional. I said I was writing it because God had done something wonderful in my life. In His grace, Jesus Christ twice saved me from addiction, and from myself. Once as a sick young man in a treatment facility in southern California, and then again as a grown man who knew better on a cold, dark country road. Following the first time, I was given the greatest blessing of all--my wife and children. Having already been blessed beyond anything I ever deserved, I was called two thousand miles from my home and given an incredible opportunity to help others. Unfortunately, I abandoned my sobriety and squandered this golden opportunity through worldly living.

Then, after being miraculously saved a second time, I began to search again for God's call in my life only to discover I was right where I needed to be. In a remote part of the country, in the middle of a farmer's frozen field, in an obscure prison drug treatment program, God used me as an instrument of restoration in the lives of a small group of neglected, abused and mostly forgotten people.

And there, in the humblest of circumstances, I was blessed to play a small role in the incredible, life-changing transformations of once-broken women, many of whom had all but given up on life. I was fortunate enough to play a minor part in shattered lives being made whole again, in valuable lives being saved from self-destruction, and in women beginning to live the meaningful lives they were created to live.

And behind all these blessings, the participants' and mine,

was Jesus Christ.

If God has done something wonderful in your life, share it with others. God has done something wonderful in and through my life. Wonderful enough that I felt called to share it with you. In fact, wonderful enough that I consider it a miracle: a quiet one, but a miracle nonetheless.

EPILOGUE

It has been well over a decade since my experience on the country road and in that time, with the Lord's help, I have remained sober and seldom encountered even subtle urges to drink. I retired from the prison in June 2017. Right up to the very end, I prayed each day for help and guidance in my work and continued to see clear evidence of His presence as participants made amazing changes in their lives.

Since retiring, I felt called to return to the institution as a volunteer. I have facilitated a Christian recovery group and presented several faith-based seminars on forgiveness. It seems the Lord is just not done using me there yet, so I keep going back.

Over the years I've developed a few thoughts about all that has happened in my life since the experience. First, I believe Christ's miraculous intervention in my life was part of His plan for me; a plan in which He would work through me to help people in need.

Second, I believe what happened to me could happen to anyone. After thoroughly examining my life and finding nothing to indicate I am uniquely deserving of God's blessings or somehow specially equipped to answer His call, I have come to believe He has a plan for each of us. I wonder though if we sometimes miss our calling because we think we lack the skills to do anything significant for the Lord. I fully appreciate these concerns (as I once held them myself), but I have concluded that if my life proves anything, it proves the Lord can and does use ordinary people to help others in extraordinary ways.

Finally, I believe no matter where we are in life, no matter how messed up we might be, we can still be of use to God. If we will just put our faith in Him, turn our lives over to His will, and listen closely for His call, He will guide us on our way. And even if we are so far off track in life that it would seemingly take a miracle for the Lord to use a flawed person like us, we can still have hope. We can have hope because Jesus Christ does miraculous things in broken people's lives every day. He really does. He did in mine and He can in yours.

ACKNOWLEDGEMENT

I want to express my heartfelt gratitude to those who helped create this book. Jim Mahon, thank you for your tremendous help and encouragement, particularly in the difficult early stages of my writing. Debbie Lange, thanks so much providing valuable help and vital inspiration at times when I really needed it. Shauna (Hall) Leruth, thanks for reading the book and sharing it with others who provided helpful feedback. Kelli (Hall) Bachara, as much as anyone you believed in me. From the very beginning you always referred to my writing as "dad's book." I wish I had the words to express how much that meant to me.

And of course, it would be ridiculous to acknowledge others without mentioning my wife. Tracy, for several years you supported my effort and listened to countless hours of ideas and concerns. Nobody could ask more of a best friend. Thank you for all your help.

Also, thanks to my mother Bonny Hall (now at home with the Lord), Alaina Landi, and Nancy Christiansen for help with proofreading. Spell check only catches so much, thanks for catching the rest.

Finally, and of most importantly, thanks to Jesus Christ my Lord and Savior. Without You, there simply would be no me.

ABOUT THE AUTHOR

Rich Hall has a master's degree in Human Services Counseling (focus on addiction and recovery). He also completed a chemical dependency counselor certificate program and is a Certified Elijah House Prayer Counselor. He worked in corrections for 32 years; with the last 20 years spent working as a primary counselor in a residential substance abuse treatment program located in a prison. Rich currently works as a Christian Counselor in the Twin Cities area and occasionally speaks on faith and forgiveness at churches, substance abuse treatment programs and correctional facilities.

Rich struggled with addiction twice in his life, but by the grace of God has been sober since 2005. As one who has experienced both extreme brokenness and God-given restoration, he believes anyone, regardless of past or present circumstances, can be healed and made new through the grace of Christ.

Rich can be contacted at twicesaved@yahoo.com

30747695R00088

Made in the USA
San Bernardino, CA
29 March 2019